FL the COOP

FRANCINE RAYMOND
Photos by Victoria Spofforth

The KITCHEN GARDEN

Published in Great Britain by
The Kitchen Garden 2014
www.kitchen-garden-hens.co.uk
francine@kitchen-garden-hens.co.uk

ISBN: 978-0-9561952-3-4

Text © Francine Raymond 2014
Photographs © Victoria Spofforth
Additional photos by Francine Raymond
Author photo by Charlie Colmer

Other books from the Kitchen Garden:
All my Eggs in one Basket
The Big Book of Garden Hens

Henkeepers' Journal
Christmas Journal

Keeping a few Hens in your Garden
More Hens in the Garden
Food from the Kitchen Garden
Beekeeping for Beginners
Keeping a few Ducks in your Garden
Peacock on the Lawn
Goose on the Green
Start your own Garden Farm
Keeping a Couple of Pigs

Three Little Hens

All these books are available from
www.kitchen-garden-hens.co.uk

Printed in the UK by Butler Tanner and Dennis, Frome, Somerset BA11 1NF

I'd like to thank the *Sunday Telegraph* for allowing me to reproduce several articles in part and in full within the pages of this book, and those I wrote about for giving me permission me to tell their stories again. Thanks too, to Vic Spoff for her amazing photos, to Marilyn, Estelle, and Clare for their sunsets, bluebells and irises, to Stephanie Rudgard-Redsell for her eagle eye, to my family for allowing their lives to be chronicled, and to my new friends in Whitstable for welcoming me so readily.

I'd always planned to leave our family house in Suffolk feet first, when my ashes would be scattered to enrich the garden one last time, but over the past few years, I've made the difficult decision to leave now, while I'm on a high, before age and decrepitude turn life here into a burden, rather than a joy.

Nearly thirty years ago, the day before my younger son Max was born, we bought a converted cart house, dwarfed by its neighbouring East Anglian wool church. The neglected south-facing garden sported an elderly apple tree and a few desultory yellow roses. We bought extra land and over the years the plot survived the benign neglect of weekend gardeners, the sporting prowess of sons and fulfilled all my horticultural ambitions. Church Cottage became home to our family, to my famous flock of Buff Orpington hens, a haven for local wildlife – including a noisy cabal of village ducks, and since the death of my husband in 2001, my inspiration to write and a means of making a living.

It's the myth I've created that has become my downfall. This casually pretty, artless acre belies the hours spent on hands and knees, not even gardening – just tidying up to open to the public. And when I damaged the ligaments in my back, I realized how much time and money went into perpetuating this country lifestyle fable, and decided it was time to pass it on to younger shoulders – and knees. Barely able to bring myself to think about a future house and garden, I decided to move to Whitstable, to the seaside in Kent, to be nearer my older son Jacques, his wife Saskia and their expected baby.

A heartbreaking garden tour, deciding what I should take with me, produced a jumble of plants that would barely fill a window box: a nut from the mature

walnut tree I planted; definitely that ruby pelargonium that a much-missed friend brought me on her last visit; a sucker from the aromatic *Eleagnus angustifolia* that flops by the swimming pool gate; and some root cuttings from my red oriental poppy Beauty of Livermore. And an artichoke – my trademark, and some rhubarb, maybe.

And what of my beautiful hens, bred through generations, whose quirky characters, delicious eggs and blowsy apricot plumage light up my life? I couldn't move them to a pocket-sized plot. The young ones with their cockerel have been offered a home next door and the three older ladies will stay on as part of the fixtures and fittings. The ducks, always opportunists, will fly off to other free meals.

On a cheerier note, I wrote in the prequel to this book – *All my Eggs in one Basket,* that if I had just a tiny garden, I'd still grow herbs, still squeeze in a salad bed and even offer a roost to a couple of bantams. Throughout life's inconsistencies, my garden has provided constancy. Now I must dream of horticultural surprises around the corner and better seasons ahead, keep fingers green, and hopes high.

This book, which I hope will inspire fellow travellers, charts my journey from Suffolk, through high spots and low moments, through family milestones and markers, sampling the fruits of our labours and meeting new friends, both fair and fowl, to a new life in Whitstable.

Francine Raymond

JANuary

1st

It's really happening. I am moving. Up until now, leaving our family home of thirty years has just been a project: an easy sale to a charming couple (albeit a Sisyphean exchange thanks to legal cock-ups), but now, finally, nearing completion, writing about it here and setting my thoughts on paper will make it all a reality.

Over the past month or so I've been preparing myself by concentrating on the downsides of this house and garden, comforting myself I will never have to do such and such a task on such a scale again. Those seasonal routines and chores that create constancy can certainly take it out of you.

With trusty sidekicks Keith and Evan, we've moved mammoth pizza ovens and memorial stones, Herculean feats that have tested our muscle and ingenuity. We've made bonfires, visited the dump, held car-boot and garage sales, selling thirty years worth of surplus family detritus from house, garden and garage, and I'm smugly pleased about my slimmer downsized possessions. The removal men have given quotes, and friends have benefited from manic fits of generosity in my attempts to fit a pint into a quart pot. I've selected the garden features I want to keep: my outsize stone walnut, my galvanized metal tree, my terracotta pumpkins – all essentials – really? Which bench of three? Which pots from hundreds? And had visions of them in my new garden, and chaos.

Like lots of people, I garden to create harmony and symmetry in an anarchic world. I'm a control freak seeking to bring order to my own pocket of calm. A new garden is a blank canvas, waiting but daunting. The frozen soil has stopped me transplanting, but a bag of compost will give me pot marigolds, love-in-a-mist, feverfew and opium poppies that would rule this garden without constant weeding. To cheer myself up, I've bought a pair of 8ft

3

metal cattle drinkers from Clarkes, our local farm suppliers, to fill with dreams of navy blue agapanthus, jaunty alliums or dark purple alliums in spring to keep me going till permanent beds evolve in my new garden.

This garden has a calm atmosphere, with simple spaces designed to create peace. I love self-seeders and wild areas, and lawns with vistas, interrupted with the odd hen or duck, but free from the crowd pleasers that many garden businesses supply to keep the punters happy. My yew *allée* with views along the lawn through an old metal gate, is a creation I'll be sad to leave, along with all the people I have got to know through my garden. May I mention the late Brian Gaught, who stoically planted all the yew hedges; my garden helpers who manfully put up with all my dotty gardening projects; my long-suffering neighbours; my shop suppliers, makers, artists and the thousands of visitors who have enjoyed this garden. I shall miss you all.

And the deer, the hares and the wild birds: the tree creepers, the twittering flocks of long-tailed tits, the skeins of geese that won't be replicated in the more populated areas of Kent. I'm swapping the pheasant and wood pigeon that create the background music here for seagulls. Until a year or so ago, I thought I'd never leave this place. It has been my life, my business, our family home – my late husband and my creation – but I'm off to pastures new, leaving the garden in good hands.

3rd

I'd like to take memories of a few last dishes with me, and though my garden is in a deep midwinter slumber, there are still rich pickings to be had from perennial winter herbs. It's tempting to kick-start spring by buying in supermarket herbs, but better to concentrate on what's growing out there now in the herb garden. Although those that survive our fluctuating temperatures, like bay, rosemary, sage and thyme, are more pungent than summery herbs, they deserve to be used more enthusiastically than the usual decorative sprig.

Try and imagine your winter garden without the colour, texture and perfume of rosemary's spiky sprawl; or sage in all its colourways; thyme creeping its way into unwelcoming spots, and the majestic bay that will, with time, grow into a productive tree. In autumn, I usually pot up a few varieties of these stalwarts in well-drained compost and stand them near the shelter of the back door, so that last-minute forays into the herb garden at dusk aren't a herbal hide-and-seek, resulting in a bouquet garni of random greenery.

Queen of winter herbs is rosemary. Introduced by the Romans, it's a robust partner to garlic and lemon, complementing meat and fish or a pan of roast mixed vegetables. Add a few sprigs to a bottle of olive oil as a standby. Sage is traditionally used in stuffings: try it with

7

pared lemon rind, pine nuts, mushrooms and garlic. Plain apple sauce perks up with a few sage leaves, and if you pop a leaf or two in a bottle of cider vinegar with a few juniper berries, your winter salad dressings take on a whole new flavour.

Lemon thyme tastes good in a gremolade, stripped of its stems and pounded with lemon zest, garlic and sea salt, eaten with grilled mackerel; or added to a winter salad of radicchio and lentils; or better still, mashed with a tin of white beans and a crushed garlic clove, a little chilli, then slowly drizzled with olive oil and the juice of half a lemon for a tasty dip to eat with toasted sourdough.

Bay leaves are best fresh with any stew, soup or roast vegetables. Add a few leaves to a jam jar of sugar to flavour rice pudding. Gather all four herbs together to make a bouquet garni, and add them to a slow cooked tomato purée with a little brown sugar for pasta dishes, or just use as a posy to decorate your kitchen table.

Other herbs hardy enough to brave the elements are winter savory – aromatic on toasted rarebit with goat's cheese drizzled with olive oil; and chervil, green and frilly, a yummy topping for scrambled eggs. Try marinating a few round goat crottins with sprigs of thyme, rosemary or savory in a jar, with sliced shallot, chillis and garlic. Top up with olive oil and leave for a month in the fridge.

Welcome these flavours, but don't forget to place your orders now for dill, coriander and basil seeds to enhance your summer menus.

*In this book, recipes pop up like songs in a musical. They're always in italics, so can easily be skipped.

8th

Last few eggs from my younger hens before they move next door to Mandy and Colin. I shall miss their fresh firm whites and dark yellow yolks, and will have to survive on shop-bought eggs for the next few months, so probably won't be cooking many eggy dishes for a while.

Have found some flat-leaved parsley and enough new chard leaves growing under a cloche of their old leaves to make a frittata – an Italian omelette, served flat, not rolled and usually eaten at room temperature – it makes good picnic food, served with crusty bread.

Pre-heat the oven to 400F/200C. Beat together 6 fresh eggs and stir in half a dozen small, blanched chard leaves, stripped of their ribs, plus 4 tablespoons of chopped flat-leaved parsley. Fry in olive oil until the eggs are beginning to set, then transfer to the oven till brown and set at the edges. Don't overcook or it'll be stodgy. Loosen the edges, put on an upturned plate and turn over. Serve cut into wedges in a crusty roll, to munch in the garden and celebrate the pale winter sunshine.

Try a frittata with leeks and spinach leaves, or chopped cavolo nero and wild garlic, or sorrel and cream cheese, or later in the season with baby peas and broad beans with mint.

9th

Ill. With all these goodbyes, my adrenalin levels must have dipped for long enough for some sort of virus to take hold. Must get better, there's so much to do.

11th

The time has come and I'm moving on Thursday. I'm still not well, so it's a slow and painful process. After a few bits of packing, I have to go and lie down and cough. Lots of help from Rena and Lynn, wrapping and cleaning, and from Keith and Evan in the garden. I'm trying not to look at anything, just get on with the work at hand, and having a temperature gives one a jaded and unreal view anyway. Can't even say I'm looking forward to seeing my new house – the hoops the buying and selling system make you jump through give little time for motive questioning. It's a bit like a really big wedding. Many a bride must have looked at her groom almost for the first time at the altar, having been totally preoccupied with nuptial arrangements.

13th

Feel a little better and want to say goodbye to my cosy Rayburn with some comfort food, a warming parsnip and apple cake, to use up a few bits and bobs before the last bit of packing in the kitchen. Incorporating root veg into cake recipes is a good way to cut down on fat and flour. Try adding grated beetroot to chocolate cake, or courgettes to fruitcake, or bake that great classic, the carrot cake.

Cream together 170g each of butter and soft brown sugar. Add half a grated apple. Sift together 350g wholemeal flour, a pinch each of baking soda and salt and a teaspoon of ground cinnamon, nutmeg and cloves and add to the mixture. Gradually incorporate 4 beaten eggs, 170g finely grated parsnip, a teaspoon of vanilla essence, plus a tablespoon of vinegar mixed with 125ml water.

10

Transfer to a buttered, lined 20cm cake tin and decorate with the remaining sliced apple, sliced thinly. Bake in the oven for just over an hour. Brush the apples lightly with a tablespoon of melted plum jam before serving, and serve warm with crème fraiche dusted with cinnamon.

14th

Moving Day, an early start and barely time to say goodbye to an almost unrecognizable empty house. The removal men come and take our beds which they squeeze in along the inside of the lorry, then Max – my son – and I pick up our bedding, the electric kettle, a bunch of dried flowers – strangely – and the cat, worried and wondering in her basket. I'm almost sleepwalking and I can't quite believe it's happening, one foot in front of the other, out of the house, into the car and down the lane, through the village one last time, and out on to the open road.

I know every inch of these lanes, and the occupants of almost every house; this place has been my life, this landscape is my home. I shall miss it. But not now, there isn't time and the cat sets up a lament that she manages to keep up for the entire journey, down the A14, the A12, along the M25, over the dreaded Dartford Bridge, and along the still unfamiliar Kent main roads.

Two hours later we reach Whitstable, round the roundabout and down Borstal Hill to that first view of the sea which

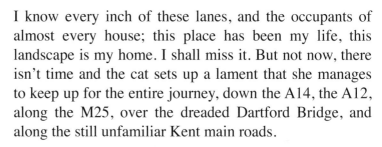

13

holds a special place in every Shellback's heart – perhaps I'll get to feel a parochial thrill for this view as time passes. We arrive in Joy Lane to find a rueful removal van, only one; the other has been stopped by the weighbridge for being overweight, so they must quickly empty this lorry so that they can lighten the load of the other, before it's released. But the house keys have not arrived, so they all pile into my car to go and have 'lunch', while I wait in the garden for the estate agent.

It starts to rain. A low moment, as the cat and I shelter, looking out on the selection of garden paraphernalia the past owner has kindly left for us: a broken barbecue, a rusty sit-on mower, a million plastic flower pots, a highchair. Depressing thoughts are interrupted by the arrival of the agent and return of the removal men. And it's on with the dance, as pieces of furniture, bags and boxes need to be found new homes. A panel is removed from the fence and a lorry-load of garden bits and pieces disgorged, then the men go, keen to get back home after a long day. My elder son, Jacques, has appeared with drill and toolbox, and, bizarrely, is attaching my carved artichoke to the newel post. And we're in.

We find a few logs in the garden, light the wood-burning stove, and sit down in the bright red sitting room to a takeaway meal. The cat, suspicious and tense, but silent at last, joins us. A toast to a successful move.

15th

Am lucky to have both my sons here for the weekend, helping make a home from someone else's till the builder comes and we start again. We sit and draw plans on the back of envelopes. I want to knock down several walls on the ground floor to make a larger kitchen, and incorporate the downstairs bedroom into the sitting room for a studio. When you work at home, it's depressing to spend your days tucked away from the rest of the house, better to be part of what's going on. I want to move the bath upstairs, but can see my sons are bemused and exhausted by all these plans and schemes. A couple of builders are coming to pitch tomorrow, so we shall see.

17th

Tax bill to pay and I'm panicking slightly, wondering how I'll make ends meet in the future without the shop and garden business. My career so far has been a random hotch potch, starting at school when the careers adviser, ignoring my Ban the Bomb badge, suggested Foreign Office bilingual secretary after seeing languages and military family history on my notes. I wanted to go to Art School, my mother had me down for a Constance Spry flower-arranging course – the compromise was a painfully long year at the London College of Secretaries – something to fall back on.

What seemed like a lifetime later, I applied for a degree course in Fashion & Textiles. I was told outright that my first choice – sculpture – would be more suitable for a man. Qualified, I designed for a couple of boutiques – oh, how that word dates me, and then set off for Milan to work as a fashion illustrator/stylist for an elegant chain of department stores. Italy was far from the domain of outrageous fashion it is today: ladies dressed in brown in winter, navy in summer, and mini skirts were worn only by prostitutes. Memories of the withering scorn reserved for London fashions by Milanese senore still leave a scar.

Back in the UK – inauspiciously just in time for the three-day week – my career path rambled on. Children's book illustration and instruction leaflets saw me through early marriage, and child-rearing days saw my cousin and I doing fashion predictions (cribbing) for the Australian shoe industry. How the mighty had fallen. We slunk into Manolo Blahnik's with visiting tanned execs in white safari suits, then on to Langan's for the free lunch, while our husbands lurked in cars round corners with hungry babes waiting to be fed.

Moving to Suffolk with kids at school, I embraced country life. Clutching at straws to kick-start a new career, I worked as a buyer at The Leaping Hare, a stately home plus vineyard, café and country store. Five years later I started a similar venture on a microscopic scale at home, opening my garden to the public, showing off my flock of scruffy chickens and setting up a tiny shop.

Napoleonic in my attempts to design most of the products myself, I published a slim volume on keeping hens. A family heirloom was sold to pay for the printing, and The Chicken Woman was born. Thirteen books on, and a minority interest affectionately exploited to the hilt, like so many of my self-employed generation, I find my chequered career doesn't seem to have earned me a pension, so my hens and I have scratched a living, till now. I love this life, a dream fulfilled, and one anyone can share: from Marie

Antoinette to Barbara Good: under the skin – however well moisturised – lurks a part-time peasant with a yearning to toil her plot. But can I make a living just writing about it?

22nd

Blue Monday, the lowest of seasonal lows and I'm standing in a gloomy hall on my thirtieth or so conversation on a mobile with BT. Why couldn't they have effected the same smooth changeover as all the other services? No way of complaining either, except to the hapless employees who happen to find themselves involved in this saga, they seem almost embarrassed – a seriously badly managed company.

24th

Well, here I am, sitting at my old desk in a new house, a grumpy cat on my lap, festooned with wires, as we try and sort the computer. Thanks to BT we were without a phone and internet for ten days. A bad time to be incommunicado – 130 emails waiting to be answered; two articles for the *Sunday Telegraph* and one for *Your Chickens* to write; and thousands of calls to make. That apart, I feel perky. I do miss my birdies, but know I'm just a dim memory in the back of their feathery minds.

A calming cup of verbena tea: verbena makes the best lemon-flavoured tea, a few leaves steeped in boiled water, then sweetened with honey, if you like. It's cleaner tasting than lemon balm and not as sharp as the real thing. The

19

tender plant needs to be brought under cover in winter, but may survive the milder temperatures here.

I try to avoid caffeine in tea and coffee, so drink fennel, mint or dried lime flower tea, collected from the trees that surrounded the churchyard next to my house in Suffolk, so each cup is full of memories.

25th

Catching up with my phone calls, am horrified to find out that my buyers had no intention of keeping my old hens, and they've been found new homes. Maybe, like me, they were up for the rough and tumble of a new life, but I doubt it. The edifice of trust that I was relying on for a smooth changeover and the continuity of care has crumbled. I had no real right to expect anything, but they promised.

26th

Out into the garden at first light to see whether I really could keep my hens here. There are no fences on the right-hand boundary, just a patchy 20ft-high privet and hawthorn hedge, with a tranche of sycamores that my neighbours have asked to fell, a rickety but lovely ancient birch, and a shed. And a 30ft square bramble patch. Who knows what's living in there? I know there are foxes about. So decide the extra move would be more for my benefit than theirs.

I'll need to find a tree surgeon and fence builder. Buds are starting to appear, and I recognize this plot is peopled largely with big shrubs, laurels and bays, and dangerously prickly pyracanthus and hollies, with a forest of damson offshoots and one or two bulbs poking their way through flooded rough-cut grass. Self-sown seedlings carpet the area under the hundred-year-old oak tree that dominates the end of the garden.

The left-hand side of the garden is almost bare earth, virgin territory left by the builders when they built the drive that gives access to the new house at the end of the garden, with a raw new fence, and a sole surviving apple tree. But the proportions are good, the garden must be 150ft long by 50ft wide, with thick clay soil, tempered through a century of use on the right, and raw clay on the left.

The area just outside the back door faces north and is covered in mossy rough concrete dotted with strangely shaped beds full of shells, hippy beads and glass, one or two ferns, arum spathes and elderly technicoloured hybrid roses. The front garden boasts a low privet hedge smothered in ivy, and gravel space to park. And on either side of the porch, a collection of evergreen shrubs that block out the light and are too gloomy for their privileged south-westerly aspect.

The garden was probably carefully tended by its first generation of owners in 1906, maintained by the second, and left wild by the last family, who used it as a wonderful playground and wildlife haven. Before the lower portion was sold as building land, it stretched a magnificent 350ft with mature trees and shrubs: a few have been left next to the oak, but the rest were felled – some lie in a heap behind the bramble patch. The garden backs on to allotments, railway lines, the golf course, then the sea, ideal fox territory. The job ahead seems overwhelming.

Cheer myself with a warming leek and potato soup, all chopped and fried in goose fat, then simmered in vegetable stock, and served with floating wholemeal croutons, topped with melted goat's cheese and drizzled with parsley pistou.

Pound a pinch of sea salt with two cloves of garlic till smooth, add a bunch of parsley until you have a green paste, then slowly add olive oil drop by drop until the sauce thickens. Pistou is tasty with any soup, on pasta or risotto, or simply spread on toast.

28th
A visit to my mother in Dorset with Max. Never an easy affair, but creeping dementia has made her more pleasant. Gone are the snide remarks and comments, though her cleaning lady, the long-suffering Iris, and her visiting carers still get a hard time. My brother lives nearby and he drops in every now and again. I can see she is getting more and more distracted. We go shopping for slippers in Bournemouth and to Waitrose to stock up. Not a success.

31st
Heavy snow here, and time to wonder if this has been a good move. Am touched by the messages of support from friends, readers and customers. I miss the community I've left, and wonder if I'll ever re-create anything similar here. I miss my house, but reassure myself that home is a collection of memories, it's not a geographical place. Not

all of us are lucky enough to have the choice to live where we want. Bereavement, divorce, lack of job or wars can all force people to move house.

I'm a nester, someone who sets great store by my surroundings, almost as a means of artistic expression. It's my sanctuary, and although my sons have flown, I want to create a new family home from home, to welcome my grandchildren. I hope, as well, to inspire others who have to make a move, that it could be the beginning of a new and exciting chapter in life.

FEB*ruary*

1st

It usually takes a period of inactivity – illness or bad weather perhaps – for gardeners to take stock and contemplate their gardens, but those planning a new one should examine their plot from every angle, in all types of weather, and preferably throughout a whole year. Start from the soil up – mine is intractable yellow clay – and work out your boundaries, check it from every aspect and decide what features to keep and what to dump.

Most of my stocktaking has been carried out from my draughty bedroom window that overlooks the whole plot with a tantalizingly tiny view of the sea, a little blue triangle to the left. I look out onto a row of new houses – garden grabbing is common in Whitstable – but sight of them is interrupted by a magnificent oak tree, planted at the same time as this house was built, and thank heavens for it.

I've made gardens from long thin plots before, mostly in London, and like the idea of dividing across their length, so that eventually the whole garden is never seen at the same time. My plan is to chop the space into three sections. The part nearest the house is for entertaining – no cook wants to walk miles down the garden to feed their guests – with a herb garden and a small-scale vegetable plot, a lawn to sit on surrounded with plants in pots, divided from the rest by a bay hedge and a pair of cordoned apples to either side of a gate that leads into the central plot.

Here, I dream of planting an orchard with a chicken run in a wildflower meadow planted with bulbs, crossed by a mown path. I want to grow fan cherries against the fence, which I hope to clothe completely with edible climbers and wall shrubs, like Japanese flowering quince – *Chaenomeles* (not to be confused with the standard quince tree – *Cydonia*), passion fruit, actinidia, grapes and figs. Also jostaberries – a vigorous gooseberry/blackcurrant cross that I'll train back against the fence as well. At their feet, I'll plant rhubarb and wild strawberries, all in sturdy raised beds to combat the clay and keep out the couch grass.

The bit at the end of the garden, under the shade of the oak, will be left to wildlife and future grandchildren – for sandpits and dens, for compost heaps and wheelbarrows, among a small copse of local hazel and cobnuts, under-planted with naturalized bluebells. This secret garden will be hidden by a fence and a sort of compost hedge made from piled branches that eventually rot down, but offer wildlife habitat in the meantime.

Uppermost in my design is the determination not to lumber myself with too much work in the future. It's heartbreaking to not include perennial beds, to limit myself to a lawn that I can cut with a cylinder mower, and hard not to show off or indulge my plant fantasies. But I hope my garden will still be creatively productive, so I can treat myself and grow those little seasonal specialities that make life worth living: pots of early spring bulbs and bottles of elderflower cordial, pullet eggs and bowls of salad leaves, posies of flowers and bundles of kindling, baskets of fruit and jars of preserves for the larder. I want my grandchildren to take their first steps on my lawn, to have long family lunches on my terrace, for my sons to indulge their hobbies in my shed (no, not the drum kit again, please) and to encourage wildlife – bar

foxes and magpies. A low-maintenance garden that doesn't mean I've thrown in the trowel.

Like most of the east coast, I can't rely on regular rainwater, so I'll harvest rainwater from the roof, and the clay soil that cracks in summer and floods in winter will need bags of grit and loads of compost to give its new inhabitants a chance, but the climate here is mild, judging by the tender almost tropical myrtles, cordylines, phormiums, tamarisks and olives that flourish right down to the seawater's edge. So there's plenty to look forward to.

I suppose I could have abandoned two-thirds of my Suffolk garden, left it to wildlife or shared the space with neighbours and stayed put, as an alternative to moving, but looking back after a childhood on the trot, major moves to Italy and back, and then to Suffolk, perhaps it was just time for a change.

3rd

Widening my horizons, I've walked up and down Joy Lane, past mostly half timbered turn-of-the-century town houses, and a few that owe more to Miami than suburban Kent, then taking a right turn towards the sea, I've come across a track that leads past the allotments to a large open space called Prospect Field, covered with trees and undergrowth that backs onto the gardens and railway line with a lovely view of the coast.

33

I almost burst into tears of joy. To have access to somewhere wild, contact with a little patch of countryside in the middle of all these houses and traffic, with access to the beach, is more than I could have hoped for. I hadn't realized how much I was missing wide-open spaces. Follow the path along the railway line to the footbridge, then you can walk along the beach, then back across the golf course, over another footbridge on a circular route, 30 minutes of fresh air that I'll attempt after breakfast before settling down to the computer. Have joined the Friends of Prospect Field, who care for and protect this space, and hope to help once I've tamed my own wilderness.

Venturing further, have discovered a fortnightly Whitstable Farmers' Market, well-organized with a good range of local suppliers, and in Faversham, five miles away, a shop, Macknade, owned by an Italian family selling exotic treats: amazing fruit and vegetables and fabulous cheeses that take me back to my time living in Milan in the early seventies. At nearby Monkshill Farm, they sell home-butchered meat and poultry, and eggs, and of course there are plenty of fishmongers in the harbour, so slowly I'm rebuilding my network of food suppliers and beginning to feel at home.

8th
The snow has come and gone and I've celebrated its passing by planting a small spring garden under the damson trees to the left of my planned vegetable plot. I should wait, but I desperately miss that chartreuse green of euphorbias, partnered with bright blue and pale yellow that augurs the beginning of spring, and a spring without hellebores would be unthinkable. Modestly averting their gaze, their flowery faces hang down, hiding their beauty, so I pick a handful and float them in an inch of water on a favourite plate. And bang goes the first of my garden resolutions.

In the background, I've planted a row of lime green-stemmed cornus, that promptly disappears against the nasty new yellow fence, so I've just painted it dark grey. In front I've put in various skimmias, four *Euphorbia wulfennii* with wild hellebores that were already here, and in the foreground, pulmonarias, brunneras and *H. corsicus* and *orientalis* that will flower and then show off their striking foliage as the trees come into leaf. It's all interspersed with snowdrops, snowflakes, arums and cyclamen that grow wild in this bit of the garden, and are ready to pick in a small bunch to celebrate St Valentine's Day.

Not so fresh from a morning's digging, the last thing a gardener wants to do is slave over a hot stove. Soups can be cooked in way in advance, then quickly ladled into a mug, to warm hands and hearts. To make celeriac and dried mushroom soup, soak 25g dried mushrooms in warm water for 30 minutes and keep the liquor. Gently fry 450g peeled and cubed celeriac in a little goose fat or butter for five minutes.

Add a sliced leek, then stir in the strained mushrooms and add a 450ml stock plus the mushroom liquor, taking care not to include the dregs. Simmer gently until the celeriac is soft. Season to taste. Then season, liquidize and serve with crème fraiche and hot bread.

Or this easy pumpkin and coconut milk soup. Peel and cube a small pumpkin or butternut squash. Fry in butter and a little oil, plus a teaspoon of ras-el-hanout spice mix (or a mixture of ground ginger, cayenne, cinnamon, coriander, nutmeg and cloves). Add a large sliced leek, and when soft, pour in two tins of coconut milk and 450g vegetable stock. Simmer gently until the vegetables are tender. Season and liquidize.

10th

Without much colour to be found in the garden, it's important to have plants flowering in the house. I bought a fabulous pot of pale green *Amaryllis* 'Green Goddess' that have flowered and gone, hopefully to reappear next year after a summer outside under a bench and a couple of good seaweed feeds. I planted a few tiny snowdrop bulbs in some silver seashells that looked pretty for a while, and have a pot of creamy white hyacinths waiting to take their turn. What next? My editors at the *Telegraph* are having trouble with their orchids apparently. Outside my area of expertise, I plead, remembering hothouse blooms in exotic conservatories where I'm known to be the kiss of death.

Then I remember, hidden away since the move in my spare room, two buckets of *Cymbidium* orchids that have made their way safely from Suffolk, and should be flowering around this time of the year. I conjure up visions of my cousin's *Phalaenopsis* orchids growing on her balcony windowsill overlooking Highgate, and think of my friend M's jungly odontoglossums flourishing in her kitchen, and wonder if they can be really that difficult.

If mine are anything to go by, cymbidiums are rewardingly independent and thrive on neglect. My regime, such as it is, centres around their flowering at a time when there's little else to cheer the winter months after the jollity of the festive season and before the arrival of spring flowers. They spend most of the year outside in their coloured enamel

buckets, watered by the rain and fed every month or so with whatever's to hand: either tomato feed, seaweed drench, and even occasionally with orchid feed. Just before the arrival of the first frosts (if I remember) in they come, to the porch or spare bedroom. As the Christmas decorations are boxed, the orchids take centre stage on the kitchen table, where they stay, flowering their socks off till Easter.

My favourite potful is greenish yellow in bud, turning pale beige in flower, seconded by a pinkish bucketful that unaccountably flowers a little later. Kept in light, coolish conditions – my thermostat stays at 18.5C/55F despite Max's attempts to turn it up, and though orchids like a tight squeeze in their pots, they can be divided after flowering, but need to be mollycoddled until they show signs of growth.

During the last century, *Phalaenopsis* or moth orchids cost more than a house, but now you can pick one up at a garage or your local supermarket. They often do quite well if they spend time on a light, but not sunny, east, west or north-facing windowsill, away from draughts, where they'll live a half-life producing the odd fleshy elliptical leaf, but rarely repeat flower. Displaying the same inherited indoor plant-growing traits, my cousin – 'You know I never throw anything out until I'm quite sure it's dead' – grows these delicate exotics with tenacity, rather than flair, and assures me that if you cut back spent flowering stems to the lowest node, they usually come again, especially if fed every fortnight with orchid feed, kept moist, but are never allowed to stand in water.

Odontoglossums look frighteningly difficult, arboreal and exotic looking with spotted throats and spectacular colour combinations, but according to M they are the easiest of houseplants for a cool shady spot away from direct sunlight, blooming away for nine months of the year, and making a spectacular show on her kitchen shelf. The flowering stems need to be cut down when spent to shoot again. M feeds hers once a fortnight and keeps them moist but not wet.

Enthused by these beguiling sirens of the plant world – there are double the amount of orchids as there are species of birds – I feel dangerously confident. With the imminent arrival of builders, now is not the time, but they seem easy-peasy, maybe I should try dendrobiniums or oncidiums or even paphiopodiums . . .

13th

We all need special occasions to punctuate winter's gloom and tomorrow augurs the beginning of spring when hens start to lay. With a small future flock in mind, have asked a friend to set some Orpington eggs under his Brahma hen next time she goes broody, giving me plenty of time to build a hen house, set up a run and look forward to starting again from scratch.

If you're thinking of keeping hens for the first time, now's the time to go on a course, read a few books, have look at the poultry press and visit a couple of breeders to see what will be on offer. I always prefer spring-hatched birds: they'll naturally grow up during the most favoured time of the year, so chicks born over the next month or two will be ready at point-of-lay in the autumn. Do you want to keep egg-a-day hybrids with short but productive lives, or good layers or beautiful pure breeds? It's worth remembering that those that lay best, eat the most, and if it's your garden that's on offer, plants will be on the menu. These hens will form the basis of your future flock, so it's worth taking the time to find exactly the right breed from exactly the right source. My own preference is for garden birds: Pekins, Silkies, Wyandottes, Brahmas and, predictably, Orpingtons.

Personal recommendations of breeders from friends are always best. The internet can give you an introduction to a supply of birds, but always follow up with a visit before ordering, to check that you're happy with living conditions and hygiene standards. I still run the Henkeepers' Association, set up to support those who keep poultry for pleasure during the bird flu scare, and I'm always happy to help our 10,000-plus members.

14th

Too shy to admit your feelings to your beloved this Valentine's Day? Then let your blooms do the talking. Of course a red rose is a token of love, but this is a mere platitude in the language of flowers. A gift of anemones may augur 'transports of delight', a bay tree promises 'unchanging affection', and camellias, 'excellence', but beware, bunches of daffodils mean regret, narcissus translates as selfishness, and privet – as if you would – heralds abstinence.

Lovers who feel they might need a dictionary to attempt this vernacular should consult a little handbook by Rob Cassy called *The Ultimate Language of Flowers*, so they don't underestimate the conversational aspect of sending blooms, and to help decode hidden meanings when on the receiving end of a floral tribute.

Fluent speakers will appreciate arrangements containing lilies symbolizing delicate beauty; tuberose – dark pleasures, and ginger insinuating desire, designed to say 'your delicate beauty hints of dark pleasure and burning lust' – so not for the faint-hearted; and will avoid a stunning bunch of delicate dried cream rosebuds that translates as 'not till hell freezes over'.

Make your flowers, and their messages last longer by adding a spoonful of sugar, a drop of vinegar, a splash of lemonade or half an aspirin in their water and place them in a temperate, well-ventilated room away from fruit bowls and radiators. Spray-mist and change their water daily.

Those caught short should forgo the garage forecourt and look instead in their gardens, where hidden away, they'll find sweet smelling viburnums, wintersweets and witch hazels (all without hidden meanings).

To some, a cake says it better than flowers, and these lovable marmalade and hazelnut hearts punctuate winter's gloom. Cream together 80g butter with 80g caster sugar and the pared or grated rind of half an orange. Beat in a free-range egg yolk – saving the white for later – then gradually fold in 80g of white self-raising flour, plus 60g wholemeal flour.

Stir in a heaped tablespoon each of marmalade and candied peel and 40g chopped hazelnuts or ground almonds. Add 2 tablespoons of milk or water and combine thoroughly. Fold in the stiffly beaten egg white and transfer into well-buttered heart-shaped tins and bake for 25 minutes at

180C/350F. Drizzle a little warmed marmalade over the tops of your cakes and sprinkle with caster sugar.

16th

Another flying visit with Jacques to Sandbanks to look after my mother who has taken a turn for the worse. She seems pleased to see us and our basket of M&S treats, but doesn't concentrate, and often dozes off. I pass the time cleaning the bathroom, because for some unknown reason, she won't let Iris clean the flat at all. We are there for 24 hours, and during that time, no carers visit her. I think the time has come to make other arrangements.

18th

Spend a day on the phone talking to my mother's doctor, social worker, and Iris. My brother and I agree we should start looking for residential care for her, because staying alone in her own home is no longer an option.

21st

James the Builder arrives with plumbers to move the bath upstairs from the scullery and then detach the boiler from the space where I'm hoping to build a larder, into the scullery. Fairly simple, clean jobs that don't take long, but are costly.

I've always wanted a proper scullery to house my washing machine, with a sink to manage cut flowers, and the downstairs bathroom has its original black and red quarry tiles and is tiled to waist height. I've also longed to have a proper larder to store food. Traditionally, a small room on the north side of the house, nowadays a large cupboard with outside ventilation will do the trick. I want to take pride in serried ranks of home produced goodies: jams, jellies and cordials, bottles of flavoured oils ready to drizzle on comforting dishes; to marvel at glowing bottles of fruit, some steeped in alcohol and studded with cloves, others in syrups made from their own juices, as well as jars of tomato and basil passata.

Chutneys and pickles are the saviours of surplus: a surfeit of green tomatoes at season's close, too many runner beans as usual, leftover beetroot, windfall apples, too much rhubarb all mixed with spices chopped onions, dried fruit and vinegar – balsamic please, not malt. You can pickle shallots, walnuts in July if you can pass a needle through the husk right into their shells, and tiny ridge cucumbers with dill seeds and peppercorns. Just make sure all the veg sits well below the surface of the liquid.

Curing, smoking, bottling, fermenting and drying, to say nothing of freezing, pickling and conserving, these are time honoured skills that have never been more topical in this fast food throwaway society. A new book *The Gentle Art of Preserving* by Katie and Giancarlo Caldesi promotes the principles of culinary waste-not-want-not and takes us through the various preserving elements: vinegar, sugar and salt, air, alcohol, heat and cold with fabulous recipes.

As a nation, we throw away a third of the food we buy, and I wonder how much of the food we grow ends up going to seed or on the compost heap. All these commitments take time, but a new approach to the value of home grown food can be built into a busy lifestyle, and evoke the joys of harvest right through the year. I'm really looking forward to stacking the shelves of my new larder.

24th

Beetroot stays in season from July to January, and often longer, depending on the weather. I usually grow the beets right over winter for their leaves, especially 'Bull's Blood' which has dark red foliage, perfect for a winter salad, and occasionally find a few beets that have cheated the frosts to back up the flavour of this tempting chocolate cake.

Melt 100g good dark chocolate, broken into pieces in a small bowl over a pan of simmering water, and when soft add 3 tablespoons of flax seed oil. Sift together 50g plain flour, 80g ground almonds, a heaped teaspoon of baking powder and 4 teaspoons of cocoa powder.

Separate 4 eggs and mix the yolks together and then into the chocolate mixture, adding 250g grated cooked beetroot. Whisk the egg whites together, add 150g caster sugar then fold into the chocolate mixture. Finally add the flour, ground almonds and cocoa powder.

Pour into a lined cake tin and cook in a 180C/350F oven for about 45 minutes. I like to drizzle a icing glaze over this cake. And it's well worth the mountains of multi-coloured washing up.

26th

I may be adapting to my new life, but I'm afraid the cat is still extremely fed up. She has become more dependent, demanding and vociferous, poor old thing. After a lifetime in one place, her territory,

I've uprooted her. Insecurity has made her dependent and over-affectionate, where has my lovely Lulu gone? Maybe, if I'd put off this move for ten years, I would have presented with the same symptoms, God forbid.

27th

Email from a kind *Telegraph* reader telling me how she moved just along the coast from here after a lifetime in the city. Like me, she spent ages looking for just the right bungalow, and finally found her ideal home – one with its original windows – a miracle in this fertile territory for replacement window salesmen. She remembers weeks removing brambles from her long garden and months trying to meet new friends. It seems her area has a young, flourishing and go-ahead WI group that has introduced her to a whole new group of people, and now she's settled in. She recommends Jo Jo's restaurant in Tankerton (a great place, went there with Jacques and Saskia last Saturday) and it seems she's marrying her neighbour. Wow!

28th

My mother has had a small stroke, but refuses to go into hospital. My brother is trying to get more help for her before she moves into the care home he's found next month, won't be a popular move. Must go down there again soon, not easy with builders here, and the kitchen walls coming down next, but my mother's firmly in my thoughts.

Keeping a few
HENS
IN YOUR GARDEN

29th

A quick walk along Prospect Field and the beach to assure myself spring is nearly here. The blackthorns and wild cherry are flowering, the alexanders are burgeoning, birds are busying and the dog walkers are out in force with their strangely similar-looking charges, racing along together. They're an exclusive bunch, but I get a cheery good morning – *de rigueur* in Whitstable – and a worthwhile habit to get into. It's good to say hello.

MARCH

1st

James has started work in the kitchen. The three gloomy small rooms and corridor, mostly north facing, are to be knocked into an open space, to let in light and create a welcoming cooking and eating space with a large French window overlooking the garden. All my boxes have been moved again to the front rooms, and a small area has been isolated with plastic sheeting, where I'll prepare food for the next few weeks in a zipped tent.

I'd forgotten the pervasive properties of ancient plaster and brick dust. It can permeate through masking tape, through plastic sheeting, into closed boxes and bags. It gets into your hair, your eyes, under your nails and into your lungs. Everything I wear smells dusty, my bed feels gritty and so is my bath, so I'm plagued with dust from the moment I wake until I finally fall asleep.

Luckily, the weather is surprisingly obliging and I can escape outside with the cat. We've set up the old metal swing seat in a private part of the garden and Lulu and I swing ourselves precariously into oblivion. I never usually sleep during the day, but occasionally wake up here with a jolt, having dozed for 20 minutes. We all deal with stress one way or another.

2nd

I can see the bulbs are coming out, I love their buds, they promise so much. My delicate cream 'Thalia', the Pheasant's Eye, that smell so sweet always deliver, but many disappoint, especially those brassy trumpets, but planted in blocks they look good, like the ones round the ramparts of the city wall in Canterbury.

Am beginning to venture out into the surrounding countryside, and went yesterday by bus to Canterbury to visit V, whom I met on a course. She has just moved to a tiny flat with a balcony and misses her garden. Not all of us have the luxury of choice when it comes to moving, some are forced by bereavement or separation to leave a much-loved family home, and then the whole procedure is tinged with sadness or anger.

Nonetheless, V believes in making the best of life and is full of enthusiasm for her new tiny garden. She'd grow plants on a windowsill if that was her only option, and has plans for herbs – good multi-purpose plants, a few salads and replaceable scented annuals in pots. Luckily her flat is on the second floor, so howling winds are not the problem many high-rise dwellers have, and the balcony is spacious and well built, though pots and soil weight still have to be kept to a minimum.

With space at a premium, choices have to be made, and V says she really has to love a plant to give it houseroom. She grows scented climbers to clothe vertical surfaces and has installed shelves for maximum pot space. I suggested trying a pocketed vertical growing kit, made from recycled plastic bottles into a long-lasting wall garden where you can even grow vegetables, and recommend *Growing up the Wall* by Sue Fisher.

At least one really comfortable chair is a must, with a perch for a glass of wine and a plate of food. Cushions can be brought out from the flat, and an umbrella is a convenient way to create shade in midsummer on a balcony. Suggest V

pays a visit to Kensington Roof Gardens, way above busy Kensington High Street, where the soil is only eighteen inches deep, but it's home to over 60 trees and a small flock of ancient flamingos.

Head gardener David Lewis told me that virtually any plant can be container grown as long as you're prepared to water daily. He suggested using metal, plastic and fibre pots with broken polystyrene packaging as crocks to minimize weight, and lightweight, peat-free water retentive wool and bracken compost from dalesfootcompost.co.uk. A piece of weed-suppressant membrane placed in the bottom of the pot will deter ants and woodlice, a nematode should be used to combat vine weevil, and a copper band to keep high-flying slugs and snails at bay.

4th

The buds are showing as the damson blossom augurs the beginning of the gardener's year, and to celebrate my first season here, it makes perfect sense to plant an orchard now and give the tiny trees an early start. I desperately want a productive garden. Giving a home to any plant that isn't either beautiful, edible, scented or wildlife friendly seems pointless, but I also need somewhere that's easy to maintain, so I'm hoping a fruit garden solves this conundrum.

Here in the Garden of England, I have Brogdale, holder of the National Collection of Fruit Trees as a near neighbour, and between us we've made a selection of trees to supplement my mystery cooking apple, an ancient and rickety Comice pear, and the aforementioned damsons.

Veiled in dust from James' excavations, with my house supported by acroprops, I keep myself sane with garden plans and schemes. I can picture two staggered rows of blossoming trees in long grass on either side of a mown path leading to wild woodland beyond. Their roots are planted under a membrane to prevent inhibiting weed growth, in a hole incorporating compost, a sprinkle of Growchar (from carbongold.com) and horticultural grit to combat the clay, then mulched with a metre-wide circle of pebbles to stop future flocks of hens scratching and dust bathing.

Looking for help to plant my trees, I turned to Appleseed Landscapes, a Kent Enterprise Trust initiative that creates employment and vocational training for those with disadvantaged beginnings. A jolly band of blokes (girls rarely enrol, it seems) turned up to move the shed to the bottom of the garden, to dig up the concrete paths and then plant my trees, and tell me why they'd chosen a career in gardening. To a man, they all said growing things gave them a sense of achievement, and that working outside appealed to them, giving them space to resolve past difficulties. Gardening, it seems, is balm for all sorts of problems.

Let's hope their energy, enthusiasm and knowledge helps them find jobs. I'd recommend them all. In this new caring society we're all supposed to inhabit, it's worth trying to incorporate hobbies with remedial schemes, because needless to say, government funding for this initiative is due to be cut. Contact your local community gardening projects for help, and some councils offer free assistance if you're elderly or disabled.

We planted quince 'Champion' – a pretty variety with smallish golden fruits and a lovely fragrance; apricot 'Moorpark', the most frequently grown variety for a southern garden, that ripens in July, abundant in my last garden; pear 'Concorde' – a Kentish variety that stores well and fruits from an early age; and medlar 'Nottingham' – a spreading tree, with large leaves, an English variety with good flavour. On the other side of the path we planted greengage 'Oullins Golden Gage' – a vigorous tree with large flavoursome yellow fruits; cherry 'Napoleon' – a local variety with yellowish cherries that ripens before the birds realize, and apples 'Red Devil' and 'Red Falstaff', both Kentish varieties harvested between September and December.

On the fence are two fanned Morellos, that flower late to avoid early frosts, producing a dark red sour cooking cherry, and on the open fence – sentinels at the entrance to the orchard – are two espalier apples Katy and Limelight, one red, one yellow. They look like a collection of twigs, rather than the beginnings of an orchard, but with a scattering of bulbs and a little imagination, I can see myself one day, sitting here surrounded by blossom, and later by the fruits of my labours.

6th
Receive news from my brother that my poor, sad, demented mum has died. Unknown to her, she was due to go into a home today, so this last fatal stroke has at least saved her from a fate she would have hated.

7th
A sleepless night. My mother was always a difficult person. She came from a generation and class that discouraged women from having careers or looking after their children, so she missed out on the joys of having

made these efforts and lived in a world whose only point of reference was herself.

So, a few final visits to Sandbanks to tidy away a lifetime. Carried to her final resting place by her four grandsons, to whom she was an occasionally generous, if dotty, gran, it's still hard for any of us to give her a resounding eulogy. We all live on in the memories of those closest to us, so it's up to us to make those memories worthwhile.

It's painful to write, but since then, even on the anniversary of her death, I rarely miss my mother, and though I can often hear her opinions from the back seat of the car or the sofa, I feel liberated from her disapproval and her countless prejudices. I wish I could have happier memories.

Inevitably, I owe my mother some debts: for my love of gardening, certainly, and my love of food. Educated at a Swiss finishing school, she spent many years living in Europe, so we ate well. She probably never read Elizabeth David, but most of her ideas would not have come as a surprise. We had foreign nannies and later au pairs who all cooked wonderful food in a post-war Britain bereft of treats, and we were blasé about home-grown vegetables and my father's contributions as another roast pheasant or grilled trout came to the table.

11th

With hotter weather and a longer season, the prospect of growing citrus trees in this country seems more realistic.

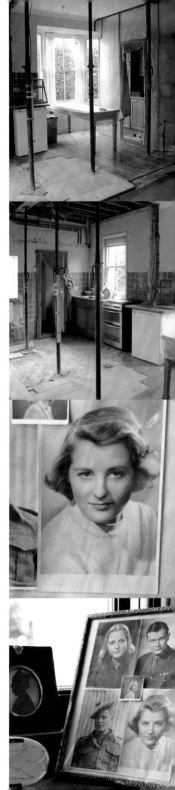

I have grown most of them over years in my conservatory – oranges, lemons, satsumas, limes, grapefruit and kumquats have all perished under my aegis. They've suffered scale insects with their sticky honeydew and sooty mould, ants, mealy bugs and leaf drop before finally giving up the ghost.

Apparently, all citrus are very nearly hardy here, and all their pests disappear when moved outside, though of course they still need heat to produce and ripen their fruit. I should like to grow lemon (*Citrus x limon*), and the variety most likely to survive is 'Meyer's Lemon'. Like most plants they like warm, rich, moist, well-drained compost in a large pot, which should be placed on wheels so they can be propelled into a light frost-free home during colder months.

I look forward to the scented flowers, in fact I'd grow them for their flowers alone, and I long for ripe lemons: most shop-bought fruits are unripe. I love their sharp flavour, the zing of their zest and drink a glass of diluted lemon juice mixed with a quarter teaspoon of powdered turmeric first thing each morning.

15th
The man to listen to on the subject of growing tender and exotic fruit is Bob Flowerdew, so I was thrilled to visit his garden for the *Telegraph*. But what do you say when the guru of home-grown produce offers you his home-reared chicken for lunch? There I was – aka The Chicken Woman and an abstainer for years – at Bob's smallholding in

Norfolk being served *coq au vin maison*, home-baked bread and poached pears, washed down with his own apple juice. Well, I just ate it all, and delicious it was too.

With thirty years' experience, Bob is the godfather of grow-your-own, in at the beginning and an evangelistic font of garden wisdom. Remembering his diktat to grow nothing that isn't edible, useful or fragrant, we toured his three-quarter acre garden – past the famous freezer carcasses, some storing apples (rat-proof and frost-proof), others topped with glass sheltering tiny pepper, pawpaw and cucumber plants, and on past potted vines, and pears cordoned against a south wall.

A man after my own heart, Bob feels more people should grow fruit, pointing out his blueberries grown in acidic soil in old baths, separated by a horticultural lavatory joke – a bog myrtle grown in an old WC – all fed with water from the shed roof, and yes, the legendary car tyres are in evidence, full of strawberries, but somehow in the inventive chaos, it just doesn't matter.

We visited the nuttery (Bob believes hazelnuts produce the best protein crop) where he also grows puff balls in late summer, then into his fruit cage made from a polytunnel frame covered with chicken wire, incorporating a pond that waters his healthy-looking potted lemons which come outside in summer. His famed use of old carpets as a mulch has mostly been replaced with geo-textile.

In his inspirational potting shed, where last year's pears are stored snugly under two vintage paisley eiderdowns, everywhere there are trials: new seedlings, experimental compost combinations and, best of all, next door in his cosy polytunnel-within-a-polytunnel, grow cape gooseberries, custard apples and pride of place, inside a further cold frame, wrapped in bubble wrap – frost-free and dry – his pineapples. His flock of Silkie-cross hens, depleted recently by one, our lunch, roam in certain prescribed areas and live happily in an old greenhouse.

So, how have things changed since Bob wrote his first *Organic Gardening Bible* – recently revised? His idealism has been tempered with experience and pragmatism – perhaps it doesn't pay to be ahead of the game. Bob and his family live frugally, with dividends paid in good health. Many others have jumped on to the bandwagon and many more have been converted. The effects of climate change are obvious and he believes water shortages pose the biggest threat to our wellbeing

And how has he changed since his marriage and the birth of his twin son and daughter, now six years old? He peevishly maintains, 'One small boy with a stick can do more damage in a garden than all the badgers, pigeons and moles in the county.' But he's a softie really, his kids have their own garden with climbing trees and he grows sugar cane especially for them.

Endlessly inventive, he practises what he preaches and experiments endlessly. And I went home clutching a pot of Bob-berry Jam, from one of his seedlings that tastes of blackberries, already mixed with apple – delicious and typically Bob – inventive, tasty, but with a slightly sharp edge . . .

25th
Tomorrow I'll dust myself down and go to Chiswick House to applaud the winners of the Gardening Against the Odds competition run by the *Telegraph* to celebrate the life of friend and colleague Elspeth Thompson.

Elspeth's tragic death in 2010 had a profound effect on me, and was probably one of the reasons I decided to go ahead with my move from Suffolk. We emailed a lot and met occasionally, she was supportive, and clever and witty and knowledgeable, the last person one would have imagined to be suffering from so deep a depression that it led her to take her own life. Looking back over our correspondence, there are a few hints: how on earth did I make the transition from city to country life? (She had just moved from Brixton to the coast with Mary, her daughter.) How did I survive the long sunless winters in the country that she didn't notice in town? But little to suggest she was at her wit's end.

Later, I was offered her column on the *Sunday Telegraph*, which I accepted with mixed feelings, so I was pleased when the paper started a competition with one of E's favourite charities – the Conservation Foundation, to celebrate those gardeners who battle physical, psychological or environmental odds to create beauty for others to enjoy. Elspeth was always enchanted by those who gardened in unlikely places, and she championed guerrilla gardening of any sort. She wrote: 'After years of travelling to write about gardens, it is by no means just the great and grand gardens that remain in my memory. If anything, I remember all the more vividly the hundreds of tiny patches – on strips of roof tops, sun-baked shingle, even the tops of narrow boats or travellers' converted buses – all conceived and tended with the deepest love and care.'

So, on a lovely day in the camellia-filled conservatory of Chiswick House, it was a pleasure to meet the winners, who were awarded their prizes by David Bellamy, and poignant to meet Frank Wilson, Elspeth's husband, her friends and agent, Jane Turnbull, and to be asked to join the judging panel for next year's awards.

29th

As James extends his empire of chaos further and further into the garden, it has been a race against time to clear a space and install my tiny new vegetable plot before the season starts. I've had to fight off encroaching cement mixers, piles of debris and that deadening dust and rubble which decorates virtually everything I possess. I usually delay any veg planting till the beginning of May to avoid late frosts, but this glorious weather has plunged us straight into midsummer – indeed this could be our summer. So I must get my skates on.

The raised beds are made. Two 100 x 250cm scaffolding board rectangles, joined with screws to avoid those corner posts that always rot, protected with Swedish paint in a lovely flat matt pale gold colour, bafflingly called Guldockra. Much thought has gone into this choice. Days of wandering about with a paint chart and trials from little pots, assuaging the frustration of being held up from more important interior work, like building the kitchen. This paint has been awarded the Eco Flower symbol for environmental safety and will grace all my outside furniture and fences.

71

With this smaller plot, I think my palette should be limited to avoid bittyness, so this hue has been selected from the house's yellow London stock bricks, and makes a bit of nod in the direction of a sandy seaside palette. The garden metalwork and house windows will be painted slate grey to match the roof.

The beds have been placed between paths covered with weed-suppressant mesh and then topped with a good layer of pebbles in a brownish colour range, and edged with a footpath laid with bricks wrested from the skip. They have been filled with the upturned turfs from the site, covered with rotted manure and then a layer of topsoil that will be replenished each year with the proceeds of my compost heaps at the bottom of the garden. With the vital groundwork done, I hope for relatively low-maintenance yet bounteous supply of veg, fruit and herbs that I really want to eat, not the usual selection of seeds that sounded tempting in the catalogue and turn out to be either too weird to grow or tasteless.

I'm planting several short rows of cut-and-come-again salads from seed. A shuffle through my selection this year includes: Franchi's *Misticanza di Primavera ed Estate* (mixed spring and summer salads); Mr Fothergill's mesclun with zesty leaves and herbs, Marshall's coriander and garlic chives and Suffolk Herbs' buckler-leaved sorrel – a gentle lemony leaf that lifts the tastebuds. Because most of my efforts have gone into producing the beds and not the plants, I'll be buying mine ready-grown from Delfland Organics who have a brilliant scheme where you order in whatever quantity you need for the whole season, and they're delivered in time to plant – this month's life savers will be artichokes, asparagus, beetroot, cardoons, celeriac, chard, leeks, salads and strawberries.

My collection of galvanized pots, buckets and bins, carefully transported from my old garden, are already looking at home in their new seaside environment and need copious watering, as do my newly-planted shrubs and fruit trees, to bed them in. A pleasant evening's chore with a glass of wine in hand in this glorious weather

Until my seeds sprout and my plants grow, I've been scavenging the hedgerows on my usual morning's walk to the beach, reinforcing my slightly dotty reputation. I have always foraged in the countryside, but it's a more challenging task here in town, but I've found delicious tiny young lime leaves (Tilia cordata) in a friend's front garden and made a salad with chopped fried bacon bits dressed with lemon juice, salt, olive oil and chopped garlic leaves.

There are several wild garlic bulbs available. The usual ransoms (Allium ursinum) are available from Suffolk Herbs with strong strap-like leaves, but I prefer Allium triquetrum with pretty white bellflowers and a gentler flavour, available from trecanna.com in Cornwall. Both are invasive in ideal conditions, so be warned.

My main course features fat Chinese noodles with a pesto sauce made from omnipresent nettles, picked carefully and snipped from their stalks wearing gloves, then blitzed in a food mixer with garlic cloves, salt, pine nut and olive oil. An interesting taste, much improved with a squeeze of lemon juice that sharpened the flavour and stopped the nettles turning a nasty khaki. I look forward to basil – and indulge in that gardening pick-me-up of looking forward through plants.

30th

How many hens to a garden of this size? I would always start with just two or three; you may change your mind about breeds, and if you take half a dozen – the maximum flock size – all your ladies will start and stop laying at the same time. I want to encourage everyone to allow their birds as much time safely free-ranging as their gardening ambitions can bear, so start with a couple – never just the one because hens are flock creatures – and see how you get on.

You can always buy in or hatch out more as time goes on, and these new birds will take on the laying mantle from your older ones, who will add stability to the flock and take on broody duties. You'll end up with a sort of chicken continuum, where eventually, as new eggs hatch, older birds will drop off the other end of the perch.

Some pure breeds live up to ten years, though the larger ladies get rather plump and only live for six. Hybrid hens are designed to have a productive life that ultimately exhausts them and can shorten their lifespans dramatically, and ex-battery hens sometimes don't survive much after their first year, though there are often surprising exceptions to these rules.

Hens come in two sizes – standard and bantam, who are smaller versions of their normal-sized cousins.

They have the same qualities, so a good layer like a Light Sussex will have a high-yield smaller version. Bantams take up less space, but are often flighty – their lighter weight gives them wider opportunities up into the trees and over the fence.

In recipes, use three bantam eggs (40g each) to two standard ones (65g): though the yolks are of a similar size, there is less white. The Kitchen Garden sells tiny spotty eggcups that'll fit bantam eggs, handmade by potter Rob Wheeler.

APRIL

1st

I can chart my whole year through fleeting smells from the garden. From narcissi, via wallflowers, lilac, old roses, lilies, buddleia, basil, walnut leaves, *Viburnum bodnantense* to Christmassy quinces – each short-lived fragrance is the essence of that season. But there is a leafy year-round backbone to the scented garden, that's evergreen, drought-resistant, easy to grow and often overlooked.

Top of my olfactory hit list are bay, juniper, rosemary and eucalyptus, followed by lavender, hyssop, citrus, cedar, myrtle and lemon verbena. Most of these stalwarts hold volatile compounds in their leaves known as essential oils, as do other garden favourites like fennel, artemisia, cistus, nepeta, geranium, sage, santolina and pine. They should be picked, crushed and sniffed at every opportunity.

Pick bunches and bring them into the house. Steep some in the stewpot, light fires with them, burn others on barbecues, display them in flower arrangements, but best of all, on bright breezy days I use them as laundry accessories to my recently erected washing line. Stretched between wooden poles is a rope (grabbed more easily by wooden pegs than skinnier plastic washing line) that's hoisted with a cleft hazel pole, so fresh air gets to sheets and towels more efficiently than on the ubiquitous rotary drier. The downsides are bird droppings (however lucky) and shower dodging, but the rainwater acts as fabric softener and the smell of fresh air as you climb into garden-dried bedclothes is well worth the effort.

Line dry your clothes to save electricity, eliminate greenhouse gas emissions, reduce wear and tear on your clothes and minimize static. Pegged properly – from the hem – clothes get less wrinkled and need less ironing – one of my least favourite household chores.

Like mediaeval washerwomen, you can spread clothes to dry on top of fragrant bushes and hedges, or select a bunch of aromatic leaves, crush them fresh and mix half a cup with a cup of carrier oil, or soak them in distilled water for a few months. Or you could sprinkle handfuls on rugs before hoovering them up, or pop them in muslin bags to layer between laundry, in drawers or in the airing cupboard, or maybe just leave them to dry in pretty bowls and make pot pourri. Most aromatic herbs will discourage moths, and many make delicious tisanes, steeped in boiling water.

Herb grower Susan Collins relies on the smell of plants when she gardens. She was just 25 years old when diagnosed with retinitis pigmentosa, a progressive visual impairment, so being able to smell plants is vital. She sells her herbs locally at farmers' markets and from her website invictaherbs. co.uk, and believes we retain olfactory memories longer than visual ones, so herbs are important for the therapeutic treatment of dementia sufferers. She gardens on her hands and knees to be nearer her plants' sensory clues, beds them alphabetically to help with identification, and thinks gardeners are a flower-focussed bunch who miss out on so many fragrant plants that provide year-round pleasure.

2ⁿᵈ

Great excitement! The kitchen is ready to have its steels installed. Single-handed, James has torn down the dividing walls from three rooms and a corridor, and supported them with acroprops. The steels, designed to take the

82

weight of the upstairs floors will arrive tomorrow, so have suggested James bring in some muscle to help manhandle these heavyweights into position.

3rd

Steels arrive, and so does James – with his wife! And between them they crank the superstructure into place.

4th

Plasterboarding underway, and then plastering: James wears strange stilts to plaster the ceiling, magically unifying all the surfaces with that milky dusty pink colour that I've tried so often to copy, without success. It's wonderful to be seeing some building work instead of demolition and dust. Jacques has come to take measurements for my new kitchen, which he'll build in his workshop.

In the past, my kitchens seem to have evolved, rather than been designed. I have ideas, preferences and bêtes noires. I need to remember that famous kitchen triangle, where sink, cooker, fridge and rubbish bins can all be accessed within an arm's reach of each other. I'll be happy with anything, after months of working in a plastic tent in a corner, kindly set up so I could carry on cooking on a building site. It'll be great to be cooking on gas – thirty years of the Rayburn, and I barely even know what fried food is.

85

I want light and space and colour, but not fitted banks of cupboards, filled with appliances I never use. An interesting side effect of living from packing cases is realizing just how few of one's belongings are actually indispensable. Lots of kitchen stuff never even made it into the removal van, and was sold before I left

7th

No word yet that my eggs have hatched, and am tempted by one or two variations on an Orpington theme. William Cook, originator of my fabulous Orpington hens wrote, 'It has been my aim to produce breeds suitable for the production of food, as handsome as it is possible to make them, and in the Diamond Jubilee Fowl, I think I have succeeded almost beyond my own sanguine expectations.' The year was 1897, the Jubilee was Queen Victoria's, and finally, over a century later, the Poultry Club has standardized the breed just in time for Queen Elizabeth's Diamond Jubilee.

New poultry breeds are as rare as hens' teeth, so one as stunning as the Jubilee Orpington should be celebrated. They're all spectacular birds: big and bold with a nosy friendliness that can only be bettered by a boisterous Labrador puppy, and although of stout and matronly mien, surprisingly energetic – the sight of a running Orpington is unforgettable.

I loved my old black Orp, with her Scarlett O'Hara flounce; the Blues are entrancing, the Whites lay the best, and though none of these lovelies has the same place in my coop as the fabulous Buff, there's a rainbow of other colours: chocolate, lemon, red, lavender and porcelain, as well as patterns: spangled, laced, cuckoo and splash available nowadays, and foremost among these, are the Jubilees. Described by William Cook junior as, 'Cobby in build, on bright reddish-brown ground, with a black bar and white spangle at the end of each feather,' this colourway is usually described as millefleur – a huge speckled spangle of fluff.

Breeders and showmen have spent years perfecting these varieties, so Mr Cook probably wouldn't recognize his invention today. The show bench has taken over, and egg production comes second place to bulk and beauty. These fluffy strains lay little after their first year, it takes endless feeding to maintain that bulk and produce eggs, and their delicious beige-tinted eggs are surprisingly average-sized.

Nevertheless, I don't think Orpingtons can be bettered as garden poultry. Their magnificent bulk makes them lazy and unlikely to roam; areas can be fenced from them with minimum effort; they spend hours preening in the sun, but when put to work on an overwintering vegetable bed, they will scarify, gobble pests, finish leftovers and liberally manure, leaving your soil the better, ready for spring planting. Visually, there's little more spectacular than the colour, movement and drama of a flock of these magnificent birds to enliven your garden, especially during the winter.

Let me give you a few tips on how to garden despite your hens. First, remember, they are attracted to worked soil, so always cover new planting with cloches or netting until plants are established – upturned hanging basket containers give excellent protection and will stake your plants as well. Newly planted shrubs and tree roots should be mulched with mats, then covered with flints or large pebbles.

One bird's favourite snack may be ignored by another, so learn your flock's likes and dislikes and protect to order, especially when shoots are young and tender. Don't cut back woody perennial stems till spring, then leave a good 6 inches standing tall to protect new growth. Prevent dust bathing in the beds by giving your flock a purpose-built dust bath under their house and keep it topped up with wood ash or sandpit sand.

Layer henhouse sweepings on your compost heap. Droppings, feathers and bedding provide high nitrogen content and are a tip-top activator. Home-raised poultry manure is not as strong as commercial high-protein-fed birds' droppings, and won't harm plants in small quantities. Keep lawns and terraces pristine and poo-free with a besom or high-powered hose. On second thoughts, I think I'll stick to Buffs, but am off to a poultry show next week, so deliver me not into temptation.

8ᵗʰ

We're planning a tea party this Easter. Time to dress a table with granny's old lace tablecloth, and bring out those embroidered table napkins you found at the car-boot sale, lay out your crockery, pick bunches of blossom for posies, pop them in a cut-glass vase and turn a welcome break into a special occasion. Search for violets, primroses, grape hyacinths, euphorbias and airy blue forget-me-not-like brunnera, they're all flowering at this time of the year and look lovely with arum foliage.

As a child in Germany, my nanny always used to dress an Easter tree. Pick a few shrub branches – saved cornus

prunings are good – and spray them matt white. Stick the base into an old flowerpot filled with sand and top up with pebbles. Hang with springtime decorations. Blowing eggs can be a bit of a chore: my friend Jane just boils eggs for hours to pasteurize them, and over the years the insides just dry up. There is no unpleasant smell, and the decorated eggs are stronger than those that have been pierced.

Try my friend Penny's almond pasque cake decorated with crystallized spring garden flowers. First, preserve your primroses, violets or fruit blossom by painting petal with a little egg white diluted with rosewater. Then sprinkle gently with caster sugar and leave to dry on a rack while you bake your cake.

Filling: pre-heat the oven to 160C/315F. Meanwhile make your marzipan filling by placing 375g marzipan, 85g caster sugar and a whole egg with an extra yolk into a food processor, whizz to a soft paste and set aside.

Cake: mix 250g good cubed butter and 250g golden caster sugar into a soft cream. Add 4 eggs (free-range, of course) one at a time, alternating with spoonfuls of 125g ground almonds. Mix together 250g plain flour with ½ teaspoon salt and 2 teaspoons baking powder and add to the mixture, stirring well. Add a drop or two of natural almond extract to taste. Spread half the cake mix into a 24cm springform tin, lined with parchment. Spoon in the filling you made earlier, and then add the rest of the cake mixture on top.

Bake for 30 minutes, then open the oven door gently and lay a piece of foil over the cake. Carry on cooking for a further 45 minutes. Your cake should be golden brown and shrinking from the sides. Leave to cool on a cake rack. Store till ready to ice.

Icing: mix 100g icing sugar with the juice of half a lemon and a little hot water to make a glaze. Pour over the top of the cake, decorate with crystallized spring flowers and tie with a ribbon.

Homemade marzipan is easy, and children love modelling their own eggs and whole menageries of Easter chicks, ducklings, lambs and bunnies to decorate cupcakes. Take equal amounts of sugar and ground almonds and bind together with beaten egg and a squeeze of lemon juice. Mix, then knead, using a dusting of icing sugar to stop the paste sticking. For Simnel cake, place a layer of marzipan on the top of a fruitcake, plus eleven small balls for decoration. Brown the whole cake briefly under the grill.

9th

When you first move into a house and garden, belongings are piled in temporary resting places that then become permanent homes. My small collection of auriculas have been hiding in the passage by the side of the house, and rummaging around, looking for something else, I caught sight of a perfect flower, compared by Sacheverell Sitwell to Meissen porcelain – one of those heart-stopping flowers that defines the season. Its face has a personality, and its palette is a jewellery box of emerald, ruby, gold, silver, amethyst, jade and jet.

In the early 18th century, groups of florists, usually men, met in pubs to show off their auricula plants. These meetings developed into florists' shows, nowadays concentrated mainly in a northern circuit. With a labyrinthine list of specs, members show their fancies in pots. Sadly today, plastic reigns, because the soil dries out more slowly, though to my mind, the relationship between the auricula leaves' farina and the muted colours of the flowers, with the weathering on an ancient terracotta pot, is one of the most romantic partnerships in floristry.

Plants are formally displayed on shelves in rows in theatres with pretty scalloped roofs, to protect them from their two bugbears: rain in winter and sun in summer. Fans of auriculas can paint and convert old shelving units, garden arbours and door-less cupboards to show off their charms. My car-boot sale purchases lead a less cosseted life. Usually spending the winter under a bench, dry, but not too cosy, I bring them out at this time of the year, tidy them up and feed them with a little seaweed. In bloom, at their peak, the best are sent for a short sojourn inside the house on a north-facing windowsill, the rest liven up my outdoor dining table. After flowering, the pots are banished to a shady part of the garden until winter, when it's back under the bench. Obviously not prize-winning blooms, but I love them.

14th

You should be getting first pickings of rhubarb. Who'd have thought that after centuries of growing in the dark, rhubarb would be the *dernier cri* of the fruit bowl, darling of the dessert brigade, poached, grilled and crumbled in every trendy eaterie. The vernal equinox fell this year on March 20th, heralding spring and a brand new season in the garden. Pullets start to lay, fresh spinach and sorrel tentatively poke their heads above soil, and deep joy – rhubarb unfurls its pink frilly stalks. After a winter of apples and pears there's reason to celebrate: it's time to spring clean the system.

Rhubarb and sorrel, top of the spring tonics, will stimulate digestion, purify the blood and wake up the tastebuds. With astringent flavours – and a mild laxative effect – both have been valued worldwide for centuries. As highly sought after in mediaeval times as saffron, rhubarb even has its own website – rhubarbinfo.com, informing us that it takes 12lbs of rhubarb leaves to effect fatal oxalic acid poisoning; and that those same leaves can be composted or turned into an insecticide when steeped in water. I even wear Jo Malone's delicious fragrance – White Lilac and Rhubarb – springtime in a bottle.

Grow your crowns in sun or partial shade in a moisture-retentive yet well-drained soil. Choose your site with care because established plants resent disturbance, and make sure they don't go short of a drink in summer. Rhubarb is rewardingly easy to grow: all it needs is a compost mulch in autumn as the leaves die down, and an occasional split to stop congestion. I love its statuesque shape and grow the plants next to *Angelica gigas* in a satisfying combination that can be echoed in the kitchen – add a few inches of angelica stem to your dishes – as a change to the usual partnership of orange or ginger.

I have planted 'Brandy Carr Scarlet' and 'Raspberry Red' from Pennard Plants, both chosen for their flavour and pretty pink colouring that lasts, despite cooking. I like experimenting with cheap liquor and garden fruit.

My larder is full of vintage concoctions that were fun to make and taste, but spirits aren't really my cup of tea. But recently, I've experimented with a rhubarb vodka that is worryingly drinkable. Take five or six pink stems, poach them in a little fresh orange juice and sweeten. Pour into a jar with a small 950cl bottle of vodka. Shake every now and again. After a week, strain through a muslin cloth. I'm not sure how long it keeps.

Rhubarb cheesecake is a family favourite. Break up a packet of ginger biscuits and mix with 100g of melted butter. Press into a deep flan dish and refrigerate. Poach a kilo of chopped rhubarb in sugar to your taste. Meanwhile, mix 400g ricotta cheese with 75g caster sugar, add 4 egg yolks, then whisk the whites and combine. Add the rhubarb, leaving aside a little of the juice to decorate the cheesecake. Bake in a medium oven 150C/300F for about 50 minutes till firm, drizzle with juice and dust with caster sugar.

That other spring tonic, sorrel, is a deep-rooted long-lasting herb, rich in oxalic acid, with a tangy flavour described by some as mouth puckering. Recipes that combine sorrel with crème fraiche or sour cream work well, because the calcium and casein counteract the acidity. Best eaten young, Rumex acetosa has pointy, arrow-shaped leaves and is perfect for soups and sauces; wild wood sorrel (R. scutatus), the foragers' favourite, is delicate in salads, but I prefer buckler-leaved sorrel, and grow it in rows in the veg patch. Its tiny, heart-shaped leaves lift a spring salad *and give a lemony hit to soft-boiled eggs, delicious with baby sliced leeks and warm new potatoes. Normally paired with oily fish, eggs and pork, try shredded sorrel with melted goat's cheese or mixed with mashed potato and smoked eel.*

Those recipes come from a piece that I wrote for the *Sunday Telegraph*, that lives on forever on their website. Readers are allowed to leave comments, and underneath someone had added 'bourgeois tosh'. A salutary lesson I try to keep in mind when writing for sons of the soil.

15th

An eight-mile walk across the downs, visiting six churches en route, eating our way through six groups of parishioners' cakes, and passing through breath-taking bluebell woods in a cake-fuelled haze. As a child, I used to dream of living in a bluebell wood. Where else would a fey child brought up on tales of woodland creatures, dressed in Edwardian costumes, call home? I'm not alone: the bluebell has been voted the nation's favourite flower. Pollinated by bumblebees drowning in a heady fragrance from nodding bells, spreading a mist of cobalt blue that hovers above a bed of lettuce green as far as the eye can see, the bluebell wood is one of nature's fleeting, but unforgettable, wonders.

Used as an indicator of ancient woodland, and once common throughout Britain in hedgerows, scrubland and woods, the poor bluebell has declined in the last fifty years with loss of habitat as the main culprit. Rogue bulb and seed collectors have taken their toll, and the arrival in the flower garden of its flashier, fleshier Spanish cousin has colonized precious home ground. Recognize the enemy: its blue anthers, pale green pollen, with florets on either side of an erect fleshy stem and curved petals, and discourage this scentless blue invader who has muscled his way in from the continent. Prevent hybridization and protect our small native perennial that can't compete in the wild.

Bluebells like well-drained cool, humus-rich soil in a bosky, shady spot that doesn't dry out in summer, so I'm hoping to naturalize them at the bottom of my garden among ferns and spurge, once the bramble patch has been ousted. Flowering before the canopy leaves block out sunlight, they should do well under the oak tree or naturalized in an old orchard, and should be planted in the green after flowering, or as dormant bulbs from August onwards. Existing clumps can be divided in late summer and re-planted 8cm deep in bunches of half a dozen when leaves die down. They seem to be ignored by squirrels, probably due to their toxicity.

27th

Today my kitchen is installed. Lovely pale blue cupboards with oak work surfaces, oiled to perfection, and best of all, my wonky old sink, a nightmare to incorporate with all that precise woodwork, but set off a treat. The luxury of a proper kitchen that's clean and perfect is almost too much. I just sit and admire Jacques' handiwork, before I unpack all my odds and ends and start to think of recipes to cook again.

28th

Almost summer temperatures, but apart from new rhubarb, no fruit in the garden. The blackcurrants are in leaf, and in desperation, I try a blackcurrant leaf sorbet. Using this method you can make sorbets with any strongly flavoured fruit juice later on in the season. Melt 125g caster sugar in 200ml of boiling water. Steep and simmer a large handful of leaves, taken sparingly from each bush, leave to infuse and cool. Add the

juice and zest of a couple of lemons and freeze in a tray. Remove from the freezer, fork over and add a whisked egg white, then freeze again. Decorate with crystallized violets and serve in pretty glasses.

29th

Another scorching spring day. An early morning run across the golf course path, through an avenue of chartreuse-coloured alexanders – the local weed of choice at this time of the year. Pretty in bud, it deteriorates with a lavatorial pong that used to make me question the continence of Whitstable's inhabitants. Back for a shower, but no – the plumber strikes again and the kitchen and bathroom are non-functional for the day. Still an interminable list of last minute jobs before the floors can be laid, so it's back out into the garden to escape the noise and dust, and control my frustration.

Need to water all the pots of plants that should have found new homes by now, but instead I just sit among the blossom and dream about what I should be doing. I need to keep reminding myself that this is to be a low-maintenance garden, and not a chance to show off and design myself a lot of work in the future.

30th

Away for the weekend, taking a stall at the Grow Your Own Show near Guildford, and my boys are laying a huge deck outside the back door. I've never been a fan of decked

areas, but I've succumbed to seaside thoughts, and instant covering of hideous concrete and crazy paving with thick scaffolding size boards, bridges the gap between kitchen and garden. And it looks good.

MAY

1**st**

It seems I bought this house without planning permission for vehicular access, something you'd have thought a solicitor might have noticed. So finally, a letter has come confirming my right to drop the kerb and protect the underside of my car. Now, we start the rigmarole of applying for a contractor, for them to contact the utilities, get back to the highways and so on. A merry dance, and an expensive one, but finally I have the validation that I really do live here on Joy Lane.

Not that I take the car out very often. One of the joys of living here is that everywhere is within walking distance, and I exercise without really noticing (and have lost half a stone), a change from deepest Suffolk where the car is a real lifeline. Have also made a life-changing purchase – a 1963 BSA Shopper, found at the car boot sale for £60 delivered. Charming, in that pale grey-green and cream livery of the period. It seems manageable, less daunting than those high-tech bikes my sons ride, and in good nick, according to Max (who somehow has a BTEC in Cycle Maintenance).

My initial rides have been tentative, with much getting off and pushing, nipping through lanes, along Stream Walk – a purpose-built ride and walkway that takes the route of the old railway line – and I'm afraid, along pavements when there's no one about. The road surfaces around here are among the worst I've seen, not that the pavements are any better. And the potholes, ruts and changes of levels make riding a bike a real challenge.

3**rd**

One of the best perks of being a garden writer is the plethora of books that thump through the letterbox, hoping for a review. Not all make it to a permanent place on the bookshelf, but one that gave me food for thought was James Wong's *Homegrown Revolution*. As he says: 'We don't eat the same food we did two generations ago, so why on earth should we be stuck with growing it?' Fighting talk. While most grow-your-own tomes repeat the usual spud, sprout and swede advice – that must by now be engraved on every vegetable grower's heart – James has concentrated on the remaining 2500 edible plants that'll grow here, and better reflect our modern diet.

A charming revolutionary, and self-confessed plant geek, he thinks it make no sense to keep producing crops that are cheap to buy, and suggest we turn our trowels instead to the 120 edibles he has trialled in his small urban garden for the last three years, testing for taste, hardiness, yield and good looks. Many won hands down over what he calls 'the wartime ration book range of veg – the preserve of the flat cap and whippet brigade'. He urges us all to take to the barricades in this veg patch revolution and turn our gardens into living larders of exotic delicacies.

Revolutions don't happen overnight, but did you know you can eat dahlias, fuchsias and hostas (the roots of *D. '*Amhurst Regina', *H. fluctuans* shoots and *F. mageanica* berries), as well as fiddlehead ferns, daylily buds and bamboo shoots? Top of his list of five star edibles is the tomatillo (*Physalis philadelphica*) a lime-flavoured tomato-like fruit that knocks the spots off the tomato, and tastes great in *salsa verde,* ketchup and guacamole; asparagus peas covered in burgundy flowers that cost a fortune in the shops; and one I've planted to extend my fruit season and confuse the

108

blackbirds – the white Alpine strawberry (*Fragaria vesca* 'White Soul'), a tiny perennial, mat-forming strawberry that flowers and fruits from early April to the end of November.

It only takes a few of these sweet berries to flavour a whole dish; I try and find a handful every morning for my breakfast muesli, children love hunting for them, and James suggests you use a dozen or so in fruit salads, stirred into white chocolate cookie dough or folded into a vanilla cheesecake mix. Try them as well with Riesling and black pepper in a sorbet or in a healthy smoothie.

Probably the healthiest way of drinking your produce, especially if you include the skin and flesh, and add crushed flax seed and oat bran, the smoothie makes a meal in a glass. Any mixture of fruit, herbs and/or veg can be blitzed, then quaffed straightaway or frozen. With a little subterfuge, smoothies are a great way to encourage children to eat food they might otherwise turn up their noses at: try apple, watermelon and mint; cucumber, tomato and basil; carrot and beetroot, or carrot, orange and coriander. Add lemon juice, garlic, ginger and chilli for grown-up versions, and crushed ice for added sophistication.

4th

Out in the garden levelling the ground beyond the decking. There used to be a brick outhouse attached to the scullery extension, with a coalhole, outside loo and tool shed. Some time between my first and second viewing of this house,

111

they all disappeared, and a huge crater took their place. I have persuaded James to fill it with broken bricks and tiles, to save skip space, and I dodge his barrows and filch any bricks that I can for my garden path.

I love old bricks, their colour, texture and irregularities. These are old London stocks: the whole house is built with them, in yellows, pinks and greys, probably made from very local clay, if my garden soil is anything to go by. Every day, I note with satisfaction that my stacks are getting higher, especially as a similar brick now costs £1.25 at the local demolition yard. I try to get the builders to reuse doors, skirting, architraves and timber, and they hate me. The make-do-and-mend culture hasn't hit the building trade round here. I use plaster rubble to level my paths and have laid the bricks in a running bond. My repertoire includes complicated basket weave and herringbone patterns, popular when second-hand bricks were ten a penny. Sometimes, they develop a white bloom, which disappears with wear or a blast from a pressure washer, but needs care not to damage their surface.

The areas not covered by grass or bricks are filled with pebbles, lugged in barrow-loads from bags at the front of the house. I'm developing interesting muscles, and am sleeping a little better: though my mind still races ridiculously over building processes, my body is dog-tired.

5th
A recuperative massage from L. Bliss, while she tells me about their plans to move into her mum's house, after first building her a small Huf-style house in the orchard at the bottom of her garden. Good plan, worked out together over the years, with visits to their local planning office to find out whether permission and building regulations are necessary. The size and position of the site and building all have to be taken into

account, but the government is realizing that creating extra family living space within your garden is a solution to housing and caring problems, so current information is imperative. A website trawl of the phrase 'granny annexe' reveals a whole industry with competitive prices and lots of help.

Sounds like a perfect solution. L and her partner want to upsize to the country and are happy to repair and conserve the family home, and mum wants to help them realize that dream, while thinking sensibly of her own future. She doesn't want to leave her home and garden, make new friends or suffer the trauma of the moving process. They'll need a loan to build the annexe, but that will be paid off when their house in town is sold, leaving money over to make any changes needed for the family house. A visit to your solicitor together to formalize any agreement would probably be a good idea too.

Obviously, a large country garden with few neighbours offers plenty of scope for annexe building, but my cousin managed the process in London. He employed a local architect with experience, who dealt with the authorities, solving the main problem: how to site the single-storey building out of sight of neighbours. Existing screening trees were helpful. A codicil in the deeds stipulates that the building can only be inhabited by family members, and although my aunt's health has since deteriorated and she has now moved to a nursing home, the space is ideal for returning grandchildren. It remains to be seen whether ultimately this extension is an asset, and costs are recouped when the house is sold.

6th

The wall between the old master bedroom and the sitting room has come down, propped with a large steel. More bricks – yippee, and washes of southern light. And we've rendered the rather dreary brick fireplace. All my non-kitchen/non-bedroom belongings are in boxes under tarps covered with dust in the middle of the room. Once the room is plastered and painted, they'll have to be moved to lay the wooden flooring which will cover the whole of downstairs. I've gone for rather bland engineered beech wood planks, far from first choice, but all I can afford. I think sadly of the fabulous wide hardwood boards at Church Cottage, and wonder if they've survived the transformation there, or are covered with carpet.

15th

Those with new vegetable beds are often advised to plant a crop of potatoes to clear the soil, and though I don't believe spuds deserve a permanent place in a small veg bed, it makes horticultural sense – and if you really love new potatoes, you can always plant a few in a barrel or potato bag in early February – remember to water well though or your spuds will be the size of peas. Coomber Earlies and International Kidney are the nearest variety to Jersey Royals, prized for their welcome early appearance, distinctive earthy flavour and soft skin, but unless you grow them undercover, away from frosts, they won't appear till July.

Simplest is best with new potatoes. My favourite recipes include James Martin's suggestion to crush them in a watercress soup with sour cream; and Jo Pratt's to boil them in vegetable stock with garlic cloves and asparagus tips, and then add a pistou of the softened garlic with mint, the zest and juice of a lemon and walnut oil.

I also love this recipe by Penelope Hands from our Big Book of Garden Hens, using home-laid egg mayonnaise – just the yolks if you want a thick yellow ointment, but adding the whites for a lighter texture, which is a better base for added flavours like tarragon, watercress or sorrel.

Break an egg in a small bowl, add an extra yolk, a teaspoon of mustard and lemon juice and beat together. Fill a jug with 250ml light olive oil, and start adding drop by drop, while whisking continuously. When the mixture starts to form a thick emulsion, add the oil more quickly, still whisking. Taste and season.

To make a sorrel sauce, add a few very finely chopped leaves to equal amounts of mayo and yoghurt, then spoon over a dish of warm waxy potatoes and quartered hard-boiled eggs on a bed of lettuce leaves. Ribbon a few more sorrel leaves as a garnish and serve. I've found wild sorrel growing in the lawn.

117

Warm, crushed potatoes do just as well with a dressing of walnut oil and tarragon vinegar and chopped wild garlic leaves; with mint, chive flowers and mild feta; and with a paste of roast pumpkin seeds, sea salt, garlic and olive oil.

17th

It's a waiting game! Waiting for my chicks to hatch today, and more importantly, waiting for my first grandchild, who was due yesterday. So we're all here poised: champagne in the fridge, bed made up in the spare room for the other granny-to-be and I'm knitting like a dervish, but of course, this little being must come in his or her own sweet time.

18th

To a broody Brahma belonging to hen fancier and writer Martin Gurdon, three chicks hatched last night; they'll stay close to their mum until they're six weeks old.

19th

V. early this morning, a son – Ludo Raphael, born to Jacques and Saskia. Little family doing well.

22nd

Off to Chelsea. That manifestation of all I love and hate in the horticulture business. The stands full of tasteless tat and garden features, interspersed with some lovely plants. It's the excess I find hard to take. Gardening with limitless funds rarely makes for good gardens. Ingenuity, creativity and consideration for nature, are what it should be all about.

These last few years have been low-key, with designers quietly reflecting the nation's mood with soft colours and native plants, inspired by William Robinson, Wordsworth and the Brontës; a romantic pastoral theme obvious in show gardens and artisan plots. Even the Big Issue seller at the gate remarked there were fewer celebs, and the salesperson offering champagne might have been more appropriately pouring us an elderflower cordial or a nice cup of tea.

The plant lists (with common names included) read like a gentle litany: sweet rocket, ragged robin, loosestrife, sweet cicely and milk parsley. Bucolic havens, shepherds' huts and vintage caravans tucked in among cow parsley, burdock, cuckoo flowers and even rosebay willowherb, grown through a sward of native grasses like creeping bent, common sedge, cock's-foot and Yorkshire fog.

Romantic cottage plots may seem cheap and easy to set up, but need careful management. By late summer, your garden will have gone on holiday and need infilling, unless you love beds of rust-coloured seed heads. You could substitute cow parsley for more manageable plants like *Selenium wallichianum*, or black parsley, or even let your carrots or parsnips go to seed.

Decked with our Press passes, we weave in and out, past the odd celeb, seeking new pleasures for our readers, until we're chucked out, put firmly in our place by the arrival of the Queen. Later, riding back home on the train, through cuttings and embankments full to the brim with fresh growth, frothy may blossom and elderflowers, cow parsley and ox-eyed daisies growing through the long grass, I felt for once, Chelsea was in tune with nature.

Before leaving, I visit the Veterans' Garden at Chelsea Barracks next door. Here those wounded and damaged by recent wars have started to garden as therapy. It's a challenging site with overhanging plane trees, high brick walls and poor soil. The project is called Gardening Leave, and I salute their efforts, offering routine, exercise and comradeship to young veterans battling against personal odds.

As an army brat (ours is the first non-military generation in three), I'm angry that while we're all so eager to hail wounded heroes, we seem less willing to help soldiers who've been damaged mentally by their efforts on our behalf. The stigma of mental illness is everywhere, discouraging sufferers from asking for help. The changeover from military life to civvy street is always challenging – I remember my father, retired and already unwell, working at a boys' prep school teaching Latin, geography and rugger – but those who are under extra stress from mental illness often fall foul of the law. Did I really hear that there are more ex-servicemen in prison than there are serving soldiers on the front line in Afghanistan? Certainly, more Falkland veterans have subsequently committed suicide than were killed during the operation.

28th

Some flowers capture their season perfectly. My calendar of essentials includes snowdrops, hellebores, bluebells, auriculas, lilac, alliums, lavender, agapanthus, zinnias, and this month, irises. Clare Kneen used to breed hens. She

sold fluffy Orpingtons, rare Marsh Daisies rescued from the brink of extinction, and olive coloured egg laying Araucana crosses. She and her birds were an annual attraction at my Hen Parties in Suffolk (you may remember them), but nowadays she has shifted her allegiance from pure-breed poultry to irises: she grows stately bearded flags, elegant border Siberians, wild *foetidissima* and scented *unguicularis* irises with the same success.

A committee member of the British Iris Society, Clare gives lectures, has open days at her iris fields at Little Walden in Essex and sells a collection of these rainbow-hued lovelies from her website (irisesonline.co.uk). I wonder what made her abandon her beloved hens and decide to grow irises? 'At one stage I was doing both,' she says, 'but it's easier logistically to sell irises online, and I still keep a small flock for pleasure.'

Clare isn't alone in her passion, judging by the number of upright flags at Chelsea. Much loved by Monet at Giverny, and though not as iconic as his sunflowers, blue irises were a favourite subject for Van Gogh. I planted a small bed of russet, terracotta and royal blue bearded irises in serried ranks in my cut flower garden in Suffolk. I loved their fragrance in giant vases in the house, but in the border I prefer the more delicate beardless *sibirica* types (especially 'Tropic Night', which I hope to plant in the dry gravel of my front garden here). The native *Iris foetidissima* with its evergreen strap leaves, striking berries and seed heads is often the only plant that will thrive in deep dry shade, and how would we know if spring had sprung without a pan of tiny *Iris reticulata*?

From arid desert to permanent immersion in water, from full sun to deep shade, there's an iris for every garden situation. Grown from creeping rhizomes, irises are generally trouble-free and adaptable to the climate in this country – in all its variations. They take their name from the Greek for rainbow, but their colour spectrum is even wider: ranging from near black 'Chrysographis' to chalky white 'Cliffs of Dover' with every shade, hue and tone between. Bearded irises come in various heights, but, like haute couture fashion models, it helps to be tall to carry off such gorgeous apparel.

29th
Next on my list of must-have plants are alliums. Few families have their versatility, with good looks and good taste; they give gardens floral punctuation marks that float above the flower border, and are partnered by a culinary team starring leeks, onions, shallots and garlic in the vegetable plot.

Given the choice, I'd plump for food every time. How would we manage without these ingredients in the kitchen, especially garlic? Speaking a century ago with true Gallic chauvinism, the chef Boulestin said, 'It is not really an exaggeration to say peace and happiness begin geographically, where garlic is used in cooking.' He was probably right at that time to exclude those living north of the Channel, but garlic actually grows quite well in this country.

Beat off colds (and close contact with anyone else) with this recipe for aioli. Pop 8 crushed garlic cloves in a warmed china bowl and add 3 egg yolks with a little salt, beat till thick and sticky. Whisk in a pint/600ml of olive oil, drop by drop. Halfway through, add a little lemon juice, then the rest of the oil. A tablespoon of hot water will slacken the sauce and an extra egg will save the mixture if it separates. Serve in a dish in the middle of a platter of young spring veg. As a lighter alternative, try crème fraiche mixed with chopped garlic chives and a squeeze of lemon.

When fresh and green, young garlic shoots can be snipped in salads, in place of their close relations the chive or garlic chive, or maybe their wild cousins, the ransoms, and Allium triquetrum, both of which make a good soup sweated with potatoes in butter, the stock, then liquidized and served with a swirl of sour cream.

I don't grow onions, leeks are much easier, so I was pleased to find the perennial Babbington's leek at Invicta Herbs. If you cut it, the plant regrows from its bulb base, and then flowers up to 2 metres high. Don't harvest during year one, so you'll have lots of bulbils to grow on. I'm as fond of alliums for their decorative values as their usefulness in the kitchen, as well as their built-in armoury of anti-fungal properties that protect other plants. For us, the alliums' health-giving properties border on the miraculous: curing respiratory, circulatory and digestive ailments, while lowering cholesterol and acting as a natural antibiotic.

All alliums make good cut flowers, if you change their water daily. Collected before autumn winds damage them, allium heads make striking decorations. I have a *schubertii*, like a massive sparkler, hanging in my porch. A friend sprays her seed heads *in situ* with purple hair dye to prolong their impact in the border.

My clay soil is too heavy to support alliums, so I grow them in my two giant galvanized cattle drinking troughs, in among herbs that enjoy the same well-drained gritty sun-baked situation, then act as foils to hide the alliums' dying foliage – though unlike other bulbs, they don't seem to mind being stripped of their leaves before setting seed.

30th

Back to the main news: gorgeous little Ludo is doing well, gaining weight, but sleeping in fits and starts. Nothing can quite prepare new parents, pale and tired. With good days and bad, they struggle on, like all of us before them. Wish I could help more.

L appeared briefly before the press yesterday. We had two photo-shoots organized with the *Telegraph* to illustrate my article on gardening safely with children (shameless, exploiting my tiny grandson), and another on the local allotments. Mum and babe waited patiently, allotmenteers waited, no photographer. The baby cried, the allotmenteers grumbled. Mistakes had been made, so a roving snapper was dispatched and eventually all was well. Felt briefly like an inefficient Cecil B DeMille.

31st

With the two front rooms painted (Steel Symphony by Dulux) and the floor laid, James and I are moving all the furniture and books back into the room, with the study to one side and the sitting room to the other. I have foolishly had the sofa re-upholstered, too early, I fear, to survive undamaged, but to all intents and purposes, in one of my bay windows I now have a desk (just need Max to set up my computer again), shelves for all my work, and in the other, somewhere to sit and watch television (ditto Max) in front of the wood burner. Almost feels like home.

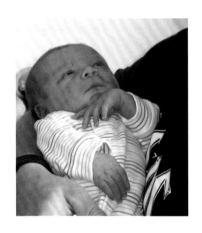

JUNE

1ˢᵗ

The garden calls. Have had enough of dust and dirt, of noise and worry, and decided to leave the rest of the house until the autumn. Email from Mrs M in Wiltshire who has downsized from a large modern suburban house in Hampshire. She and her husband are ex-henkeeping course pupils finally living the dream, having moved to a tiny Grade II listed, timber-framed cottage with no mod cons. She's been cooking in the dining room on a slow cooker balanced on top of a tumble dryer for the last year, fetching water and washing up in the bath upstairs. (I remember doing the washing up in the shower in March, and thinking how good it was to rinse with the shower attachment, so have bought a tap for the kitchen sink with a pull-out rinser.)

Mrs M now has a kitchen with an aubergine Aga, and they have slowly renovated the rest of their house, sorting out their belongings in boxes, but have left the bathroom till winter and are working on their garden too, asking advice on where to site the chicken run. She ends her email saying 'Still lots to do, but sometimes you have to go with your heart. It was our last chance to change our lives, and so we took it. The village is friendly, with lots going on and we hope that by this time next year, we'll have a nice garden with three hens to delight us and our grandchildren, our cottage will at last be ours and we can get on with living in it and sharing it with friends and family, rather than working in it. But don't let anyone tell you it's an easy option or that life will be cheaper.'

Change is never easy, and shouldn't be left too late in life. It takes physical strength and mental adaptability to move house – and it's good to have a little energy left over to join in the new community as a driver, rather than a passenger. There will always be a period of lonely transition, lost wandering in no-man's-land. Making new friends can be difficult. I joined a book club, the local Horticultural Association, supported local causes, but was lucky to have acquaintances and part of my family already here.

I still spend time wondering if I made the right choice, missing my network of friends and their support, nostalgic for a landscape I knew like the back of my hand and familiar faces at every turn. But Whitstable is a jolly sort of place with plenty going on – voted 16th in *The Times'* Best Place to Live competition – and with a local email link – the Whitternet – that trumpets anything of interest.

I've been lucky too with my neighbours: most came and introduced themselves, some with welcome bottles of wine and invitations, and a few have become real friends. On the first year anniversary of my move, I gave a small party and was able to muster a reassuring crowd for fizz and cakes. With plans to renovate the house and garden taking up headspace, I think I was too busy to be miserable, and by the time I had a moment to think about it, the worst was over and the metamorphosis complete. We all get our confidence from the roots up, but it takes time to establish a new root system.

A celebratory strawberry fizz can be made easily with frozen or fresh fruit blitzed with sugar and rosewater to taste and topped up with prosecco. Add a festive rim to the glass by dipping the edge in a saucer of diluted rosewater, then in a circle of caster sugar and decorate with rose petals.

3rd

A lawn – or not? Mowing the lawn is a chore, one that I've avoided for the past couple of decades. Originally it was my husband's only regular involvement with the garden in the general division of labour, then a chore delegated to teenage sons – who though not enthusiastic, were at least keen on the financial rewards; finally it was part of my helping hand in the garden – Evan's – weekly routine. I quite like mowing, it's an instant visible improvement, and I love the smell of cut grass, but large, efficient, fuel mowers need upper-body strength. How dare manufacturers produce mowers that half the country's gardeners can't even start?

A garden needs the visual restfulness that an area of green sward provides, a counterpoint to all that busy planting, a different texture, somewhere to sit, to play, to lie on a rug and watch the sky. In this new garden, I want to avoid needing regular gardening help for as long as possible, but I'd like somewhere for Ludo to attempt his first steps, somewhere soft to try his first bike and somewhere to kick a ball, so I've laid out a rectangle, weeded, dug and raked the soil, and raised the level to reach the brick paths with several bags of topsoil from the local builders' merchant. I've seeded with a special kid's play mix containing rye, creeping fescue and some brown top bent, that'll be hard-wearing but good looking.

After seeding and a light rake, I've performed that strange side-stepping lawn layer's dance, while praying for rain.

137

Needless to say, I still had to water the lawn nearly every evening until its first gentle cut with my vintage cylinder lawn mower. I whirr up and down this grassy area, and then through the meadow to the end of the garden. It takes less than 15 minutes, but eventually I'll have to mow further inroads, so I can beat a path through the long meadow grass to the washing line and the swing seat, especially when it's wet. I rake up my cuttings – good for the waistline and the lawn, and lay them in a thick layer over the compost heap to warm up the contents, and speed up the decomposition.

5th

Arrival of three galvanized 150-gallon water cisterns from eBay, to collect rain from the house, garage and shed roofs. Ah, the vagaries of the British weather! Whether you live in the wet west or in the arid east, water is a precious commodity. Over the past few years, June seems to have exhibited the widest array of weather conditions. One day we're baking hot and sunbathing, the next sheeting rain and a fire in the grate. When there's a drought, gardeners are always clobbered first and there is talk of charging us for our water, so some kind of water saving in the garden makes sense, to water the plants, wash the car and clean the terrace, and oh, the joys of soft water.

I saw a lovely pair of call ducks for sale the other day, I was very tempted – but have promised my family never to fall again. Those who remember my paddling dabbling 200-bill-strong flocks in Suffolk will understand why. But I really miss my ducks with their interminable broods and friendly faces. If I got two call drakes, they wouldn't call, and they could wander round the garden and eat the snails . . . enough, my chicks will be here soon.

6th

Looking in the mirror, I wonder if anyone from my past life would recognize me. Let me explain. Have found an excellent French lady who cuts my hair. OK, I admit to having a few blonde streaks discreetly added to give the impression of sunnier times. Pascale has performed this task several times, successfully, then one morning, chatting away, my hairdressing was taking much longer than usual. A little *distraite*, Pascale had coloured my entire head blonde. So now I have long blonde hair and I seem to have developed a tan working away in the garden. Very strange, not sure it was quite my ambition to look like this.

7th

Writing a tale of two berries for my column. One, the strawberry, is ubiquitous – somehow diminished by its own success – and in demand throughout the year; the other is near extinction and now almost entirely the preserve of gardeners. The future of the gooseberry is in our hands. It hasn't always been a neglected fruit. Admired by some for its zesty oomph and lauded by Culpeper, Tusser and Turner, this hairy berry was at its peak during the mid 18th century and popular among cottage gardeners, whose ambition was to grow larger and larger berries, a process that often seems to herald decline.

Like apples, gooseberries come in cooking and eating varieties. With little space now, I grow four dessert berries as sentinels at each corner of my new raised fruit bed, and I use the thinnings (picked to encourage bigger berries) in the kitchen. They grow best in rich soil in a sunny site, I keep them mulched and well watered, and prune in November to encourage air circulation, cutting back the previous year's growth to two buds. Goosegogs have an affinity with elderflower and sweet cicely:

both help reduce their mouth-puckering acidity and are at their best now.

A marriage made in heaven, tart green gooseberries and aromatic elderflower. This jam will fill tarts for parties, make a sauce for steamed puds, or a filling mixed with crème fraiche in a sponge cake, decorated with tiny elderflowers dipped in egg white and dredged with caster sugar for a summer birthday.

Top and tail 350g gooseberries, pop them in a pan with a pint/300ml of water and 3 elderflower heads wrapped in a muslin bag. Simmer till the fruit is soft. Remove the flowers and slowly add 450g granulated sugar. Stir till dissolved, then turn up the heat to fast boil until setting point is reached. Cool and pour into jars. Label and store.

Gooseberry fool is heavenly. Nigel Salter likes the crunch of the unsieved seeds in his; Delia uses Greek yoghurt in hers; Lotte Duncan uses custard and elderflower cordial and I like a mix of one part mashed sweetened berries to one part custard and one part thick whipped cream. This mixture can be frozen to make ice cream.

Use gooseberries mixed in cakes, in muffins and crumbles with chipped macadamia nuts, swirl them with crumbled meringues and cream in an Eton mess, or poach them with chopped sage leaves to make a sauce to go with mackerel or pork.

On the other hand, there's no taste quite like that of an English strawberry that's been sun-ripened on the plant. For many the only good strawberry is one that has been grown to full ripeness, harvested and eaten that same day, so eschew all those foreign berries, grown in polytunnels all through the year, and plant a few 'Florence', 'Norfolk Nectar' or 'Mara des Bois' – a berry with the size and yield of modern cultivars but with all the flavour of wild berries.

Dorothy Hartley, writing in 1954, suggests this recipe in her book Food in England. Take a deep bowl full of lightly whipped cream, drop in as many strawberries as it will hold, stirring and mashing slightly as you go and when the cream really won't take another berry, leave it to stand for half an hour. Crust it over with dredged white sugar and 'serve in June on a green lawn, under shady trees'. Let's rediscover the glory of those berries.

I confess to liking strawberries sprinkled with a few drops of good balsamic or sherry vinegar, with a couple of twists of good black pepper, or a scattering of little coriander flowers. Everyone likes them frothing in a glass of champagne, or dipped in melted white chocolate. Late season's berries can be made into sorbets, adding the juice of half a lemon; into fridge jam, combining 150g sugar with a kilo of fruit, then simmered for half an hour and packed in jars into the fridge for quick consumption; or mashed into a purée and frozen for winter puds (whole strawberries freeze into an unappetizing mush).

143

10th

Showing a tiny baby round my garden fills me with joy and a weight of responsibility I don't remember feeling with my own sons. I long to help and be a useful grandma, but am terrified of looking after such a precious bundle. I imagine sharing my garden with this tiny person, and long to pass on my love of plants, but shudder at the dangers lurking up my garden path.

Parents develop strategies to stay sane with just one eye open that I'd never dare as a grandparent, though, of course, we only have to stay vigilant in short bursts. Jumping the gun a little, I did a little research into gardening with toddlers with my nice new neighbour Kirstie and her son Harry. It seems a minefield. But I'm convinced playing outside is important for good health and a hearty immune system, apart from being enormous fun. For babes in arms, like Ludo, just a wander round will be perfect, pointing out favourite plants and pretty colours, sniffing perfumes and herbs, listening to the birds and insects, feeling the sun and the wind while we sit on the rug on the lawn during long summer days – with sunscreen and sunbonnet, of course.

A slightly older baby would enjoy a game of who likes butter, when a buttercup is held under the skin and its reflection shines on chubby cheeks. But no, buttercup stems irritate the skin, and if eaten will cause stomach ache, and of course, butter is high in cholesterol. Maybe we could plant some bulbs in pots and watch them grow. Stop now – daffs, hyacinths, crocus, snowdrops – all deadly poison. Anxiety levels rise as I imagine encouraging an early interest in vegetable growing: planting runner beans (choking hazard); growing alpine strawberries (watch out for allergies); or cherry tomatoes (no, the stems and leaves are poisonous). I long to pass on my love of foraging, but shiny berries: privet, ivy, holly and yew look just as tempting as a strawberry. And then I remember the First Rule for Gardening with Children: do not to allow them to eat anything without asking permission first.

Subsequent rules include keeping certain areas out of bounds without supervision: tool sheds, greenhouses, and water (unless covered with weldmesh). Watch out for dog and cat poo (especially in sandpits and raised beds), and rabbit, bird and chicken poo on shoes. There is a long and daunting list of poisonous plants on the RHS website, but a garden devoid of these plants would be a soulless place.

Reminding myself that, somehow despite these perils, my own children survived our garden, I think of the fun we had making cress-heads by planting seeds in empty eggshells; designing moss gardens on trays, and watering our vegetables with water pistols. I remember following snail trails, making daisy chains, racing woodlice, and whole seasons were passed poking ants' nests.

We had picnics everywhere. Even now, any occasion is worth packing a basket and heading for the bottom of the garden, at least. I've watched Harry next door spend hours following his father round their garden with a small plastic mower. All boys love being outside before they reach the duvet years, when the mere thought of fresh air elicits a grumpy snort, but recently watching my sons in small gardens of their own, those gardening genes are winning through.

For picnics and parties, homemade jelly is easier than you think and you can avoid the artificial colourings and flavourings guaranteed to make

children's parties go with a bang. For a really pretty jelly float some blueberries or blackcurrants in the mixture before it sets.

Put 6 tablespoons of very hot water into a bowl and sprinkle in a sachet of gelatine or agar agar, if you're vegetarian. (Always add the gelatine to the water – not the other way round). Leave for a few minutes, then stir until dissolved. Take a pint/600ml measuring jug, pour in the jelly mix and top up with fruit cordial or any other fruit juice diluted to taste. Leave to set in the fridge.

To turn jellies into a grown-up treat, try adding a little liqueur to the mixture. I'm fond of blackcurrant with crème de cassis, or limoncello with lemon jelly and blueberries or cherries and kirsch. If you whisk the jelly before it sets, you'll get a pretty bubbly effect.

To make a quick fruit-flavoured ice cream to go with your jelly, add a spoonful or two of homemade jam to a good vanilla ice cream.

23rd

It's a dozen or so years to the day since my husband died suddenly. No longer an acutely painful memory, it's still a time of sadness and regret, so we cheer ourselves up and mark the anniversary of his death with a jolly outing to somewhere my sons and I know he would have enjoyed. An old hippy at heart, he would have loved Whitstable with

its holiday atmosphere, and the sea – he was a keen sailor. So, since Ludo's birth we have chosen to celebrate Jean's life on the beach with a family party in one of the huts on West Beach.

West Beach is along from the main drag, on the way from Whitstable to Seasalter. Just a few minutes from my house along a track, and its huts interplanted with roses, honeysuckle and broom. Visitors rarely seem to be bothered to trek out this way, there are no pubs, restaurants or amenities, so it's a peaceful spot to spend time, especially during the week. At weekends, some of the multi-coloured huts come to life and families have parties, make bonfires, play music and enjoy the seaside, but most of the year these pretty wooden cabins lie dormant, and some never see the light of day. Year in and out they stay locked as ivy grows over them and they slowly decay. It's such a waste.

I nearly bought a hut as I arrived, but foolishly demurred. Two years on the price has doubled. So we rent from a friend, camping and cooking, and enjoy every minute, sometimes crouching behind windbreaks and dodging the showers, but often revelling in the sunshine. Sometimes we pack a quick meal and occasionally we have a proper party.

Everything tastes better outdoors. If you're walking, travel light. We have a Harrods hamper with matching picnic ware that takes a team of sherpas to transport, but for a

149

spur-of-the-moment al fresco meal, sling a rug over your shoulder, grab a basket packed with an impromptu meal and head off. Pack a sharp knife and a small loaf – a ciabatta with inside hollowed out and packed with salad, goat's cheese and basil. Add a bunch of radishes with some soft-boiled bantam or quail eggs to dip into sea salt mixed with black pepper and roast cumin seeds, and a bag of fruit.

For a celebratory meal, we take our fire-bowl down to the beach. We eat bruschetta rubbed with garlic and olive oil and covered in mashed baby artichoke or tomato passata and basil to start with; then grilled halloumi and red onion kebab to follow, covered with my favourite new beetroot and walnut relish. Based on a recipe by John Torode, blitz together 4 boiled beetroots, 4 fried shallots, a handful of walnut pieces, a teaspoon of rose harissa with a little balsamic vinegar and walnut oil. Season and conserve by adding a layer of oil.

Anything cooked in foil works well on the grill. We love halved stoned peaches or nectarines covered in brown sugar with vanilla essence and dotted with butter and a little peach brandy, folded in foil and popped on the grill for 15 minutes. And we toast JF's memory with local fizzy wine from one of Kent's vineyards.

The six foot slate standing stone memorial (which stood sentry by the swimming pool in Suffolk that Jean-François helped to build and loved dearly) was manhandled here with great gusto by a team of removal men, and has now been relocated near an ancient apple tree in the new garden. It's comforting to have it close to hand; not everyone wants to be remembered in a churchyard. A garden surrounded by favourite plants is as near to heaven as I shall get. While the comforting properties of gardening as therapy are well trumpeted, the solace of being in a garden surrounded by plants and memories is often overlooked.

29th

My daily walk along the beach is full of lovely smells. I try to sniff a different rose every day, from other peoples' front gardens and parks, but not yet from my own. Roses are fairly hideous plants for most of the year. With twisted thorny stems that grab your clothes and snag your hair; their foliage is often discoloured and diseased, but for this month of the year, they are worth the other eleven. I thought I could forgo that month-long charm, but have succumbed and decided to buy 'Souvenir de Docteur Jermain' with deep magenta blooms and a delicious aroma to clothe one wall of the chicken run. I prefer climbing and rambling roses, but now have two standard roses in salmon pink in my front garden that seem to flower their socks off most of the year, just to annoy me. I can't quite bring myself to dig them up, but we'll move them into the hedge where they must take their chances.

Frances Bissell's The Scented Kitchen is a book I keep close. She gives a recipe for rose petal jelly using a kilo of cooking apples and 600ml of dark red rose petals, and suggests we finish our meal on an elegant note 'a rose vacherin: a meringue on each plate, a layer of whipped cream, a quenelle of good ice cream on top, a spoonful of rose petal jelly and a crystallized rose petal to finish it'.

To make jelly she tells us to wash and chop the apples and put them and their skin and peel in a saucepan. Cover with water and cook till soft. Mash to extract as much fruit and pectin as possible then strain through a jelly bag overnight.

Measure the volume of the jelly and then match it with sugar. Pound half the petals with a little sugar and mix with the juice and the rest of the sugar. Heat in a saucepan and stir till the sugar has dissolved. Add the remaining petals and boil. Boil fast till setting, then pot in small jars.

Compare this jelly with rose petal jam where 200g of dark red damask rose petals are placed in a bowl with 250g of caster sugar and the juice of a lemon. Mix by hand to a paste. Dissolve 250g of sugar in a saucepanful of 500g water, add the petal mixture and boil for about half an hour till syrupy. Delicious spread on toasted brioche.

30th

A present of a box of blue eggs from a new friend, who is trying to breed a better blue egg-laying hen. As a doctor, she has just the right sort of scientific brain to cope with the mysteries of genetics. Different breeds lay different coloured eggs: they can be shades of brown, white or blue. Birds with white earlobes and Mediterranean origins lay white eggs, those from South America lay pale blue/green ones; Welsummers, Marans and Barnevelders lay dark brown eggs, but most other breeds lay a lovely pale beige-tinted egg.

Hybrid breeders, like my friend, have manipulated pure-breed genes from the best laying varieties like Rhode Island Reds, Light Sussex, Leghorns, Marans and Araucanas

to produce a range of coloured egg laying hybrid hens available to back-garden henkeepers.

The colour of the egg's shell makes no difference to the flavour of the egg – that's determined by what your hen eats. The lovely deep yellow of a home-raised bird's yolk is affected by the amount of greenery consumed, and in batteries by the yellow dye added to her feed. If your flock doesn't get enough of the right food there will be few eggs. Like us, they need protein for energy, warmth and the repair of cells. It's the surplus food that provides those delicious eggs.

155

JULY

4th

Max has come down from London, with his carpenter friend Liam, to build a garage to house his precious beach buggy. Started in his late teens, not long after the death of his dad, and built from scratch on an old VW chassis, this project has seen him through all sorts of trauma, from broken hearts to mind-numbing stopgap jobs. It has taught him to weld, make parts from nothing, build an engine, and raise funds – mostly from me – and is now in its third incarnation. Each time, the buggy passes its MOT first go, with much applause, it goes on several salutary journeys, and then somehow falls short of ridiculously unrealistic expectations, and is rebuilt.

The buggy's last outing took Jacques to his wedding in some style, but since then it has lived in a friend's barn, waiting to find a new home here in Whitstable. So, I've cleared a shrubbery from a plot to the left of the house, and James has built a plinth and ramp, a pair of brick piers and hung a garage door. Between the two of them, Max and Liam have raised a timber frame over the weekend – incorporating an old door and window left over from the house – with incredible speed, thanks to Liam's professionalism and Max's enthusiasm, fuelled and cheered on by this take on the builder's bacon sarnie: broad bean, artichoke heart, bacon and ricotta bruschette.

Only a few broad beans left, so they've been podded, peeled and added to a jar of artichoke hearts, then mixed with a tub of ricotta cheese and topped with fried bacon. Halved lengthwise, rubbed with garlic and drizzled with olive oil, two ciabatta loaves have been toasted, and spread with the seasoned mixture. Just as good on focaccia or in pitta breads.

Monday finds Max and his new mate – me, cladding the garage frame with timber boards, putting on an Onduline roof and ridge, and attaching bargeboards and guttering. Just a week on, Max has gone back to London, and with muscles I never noticed before, I'm left painting a new garage in house colours of sand and slate. I'd be quite happy to live in a slightly larger version of this building, but the buggy has been delivered with much fanfare and will live there in solitary splendour, as befits a vehicle that has probably cost as much as a Ferrari.

6th

Exciting day, my lovely Orpington chicks arrive chaperoned by their handsome Brahma mum (kindly lent by their breeder Martin), they've settled in seamlessly, enjoying their surroundings and faultlessly blending in with the local colour scheme. Now I know why I've been painting everything in the garden that particular soft apricot yellow – I must have been missing that special Buff Orpington hue.

For almost the first time since I moved – sitting and watching my small flock fossicking around the orchard – I've relaxed in the garden. Fellow henkeepers will know exactly what I mean: idling watching your birds is bucolic bliss.

7th

Not all aspects of keeping hens are problem-free though. By now, some henkeepers may well be watching spring-

£2.50

hatched chicks sideways with trepidation. Pullets or cockerels – laying hens or crowing cocks? Pullets tend to hold themselves more horizontally than the cockerels' upright stance, and strangely seem to have more feathers in the tail department, as well as smaller crests. In some breeds, like Pekins, young cocks show their sex early with precocious crests; some, like Brahmas, with longer legs, others like my Orpingtons can be a conundrum until they crow. If, at 12 weeks, you take a piece of card and slide it under their neck feathers, the females have round-ended feathers, and the boys, pointed. I know established breeders who have made mistakes – a good reason never to buy tiny chicks.

I was suspicious of our third chick the minute I set eyes on him. I'd never planned to keep a cockerel here in this suburban neighbourhood anyway, so he can stay a little longer and go back to the breeder with his mum in October, as promised. He will take a little longer to mature than his sisters who'll be fully grown at six months. If he spots competition, he can repress his sexuality and not utter a crow or display a comb. A cockerel, moi? Even without another cock about, this one would do well to keep a low profile. A neighbour has threatened to get his gun out if he hears a cock-a-doodle-doo. Can't say I really blame him, but oh, the joys of living on the Kent/Miami borders . . .

On the subject of cockerels, I remember the last bird I hatched in Suffolk – a spoiled only chick, who at six weeks was suddenly abandoned by mum who

163

went broody. Dad immediately took over, feeding, caring, sleeping with the tiny chick under his wing, till it was more than obvious that he too was a cockerel. So there are New Men even in the chicken run.

11th

Nosing down the road between nearby Graveney and Faversham, I passed a sign: 'Cherries First Right'. Unable to resist such an invitation, I turned into School Farm's drive, meandered down a track, through conventional apple and pear orchards, and just as I was thinking this was the fruity equivalent of a wild-goose chase, I found myself back in H E Bates country, in a cathedral of standard cherry trees supporting 50ft ladders and a sales booth proclaiming 'Terry's Cherries – sound your horn for service!'

From this dreamland of fifties' Kent, when children tucked bunches of cherries behind their ears and picnicked in orchards among beehives, Terry sells nine varieties of cherries, from Early Rivers to Nobles, with Merton Blacks and Glories, Noir de Guben (known locally as Nardy Gordons), Vans (Terry's favourites), and Stellas, Napoleons and Gauchers in between, all fruiting in turn over the six-week season.

He sets up home with his stove and kettle in the orchard in late June, to keep the birds off his precious crop as it ripens, with various Heath Robinson bird scarers: ropes, pulleys and football rattles, all set in motion from his camp. After a lifetime's battle against the birds – Terry started 'birding' as a lad on a motorbike, raging up and down the rows of trees – he won't shed a tear at the reported demise of the starling.

As with most good things, cherries made their way here via the Romans (many a Roman road had cherry trees along its length, sprouted they say, from stones spat out by marching legions) and their cultivation was continued first by monks, then after the dissolution of the monasteries, by large estates. Henry VIII ordered cherry orchards to be planted here, where they continue to be clustered, enjoying the well-drained soil (in parts) and sheltered climate.

Terry shins up his cherry trees with all the nimble insouciance of a steeplejack, but it's their height that has heralded their decline, and these glorious standards have been superseded by rows of netted bushes on dwarf rootstock, pollinated by cardboard hives of imported bumblebees. With the grubbing up of ancient cherry orchards, expensive imports took over, but now a few English growers are fighting back. If you want to reach your fruit, a six-foot tree makes sense, but if like me you hanker after the romance of a standard, the National Fruit Collection at nearby Brogdale will graft you one, given a year or two's notice. And a tapering cherry picking ladder can be found in the junkshops of Whitstable, if they haven't been cut down too, to use as towel rails.

The English cherry season is short, so enjoy them while you can. Best eaten straight from the tree, but if your purchase makes it home, serve in a bowl of iced water with chunks of ice. Traditionally cherries are partnered with chocolate, but even the thought of a Black Forest gateau makes me shudder. Dip them in bowls of melted white and dark chocolate if you must, but I prefer them sieved in a coulis then poured over vanilla ice cream, pitted in a cherry Eton mess or soaked in Kirsch in a deep batter clafoutis.

Make your own cherry brandy by filling a jar with perfect fruit up to a third full, add one third sugar and top up with cheap brandy. Dissolve the sugar by shaking the jar occasionally, then leave to mature for three months. Cheers Terry!

15th

Falling for that old garden cliché – the lavender-lined path smelling sweetly as you brush past (only beaten by rose framed doorways and honeysuckle arbours) – I have ordered my plants from a local nursery. Lavender is the ultimate multi-purpose plant: a horticultural Swiss army knife of a shrub, combining fragrance and flavour, elegant looks and drought-beating characteristics. I have chosen 'Grosso', an intermediate lavendine, a hybrid between *officinalis* and *latifolia*, now grown commercially with dark blue flowers and exquisite scent. It flowers late in the season and is easy to keep compact – just a quick shave of stems after flowering, and at 90cm tall, it's a tempting thought for my front garden, planted in gravel.

Documented historically for more than 2000 years and used to mummify, to protect from the plague and to perfume, lavender's properties are legendary. Elizabeth I used it to ease her migraines, Victoria to scent her linens and the Shakers and Quakers were lavender kings. Lavender flowers make lovely confetti; I keep a bunch tied with ribbon on my pile of drying-up cloths, and a bucketful of stems in the loo (to dry lavender, bunch together and hang upside down in a

cool dark place). Despite being nectar-rich and attractive to bees, branches were used to repel insects, especially fleas.

Now everywhere on the trendiest of menus, lavender (used sparingly) can be substituted in recipes wherever you might have added rosemary. Best picked fresh from the garden – dried lavender is stronger but has a dusty texture – from home grown plants that have not been sprayed. I like the flavour of English angustifolia varieties that have a lemony tang and are sweeter than the more camphor-smelling latifolias or hybrids. I only use the buds, bruising them with a mortar and pestle, then sprinkle parsimoniously. You can have too much of a good thing.

Try popping lavender buds in your sugar jar for a few weeks then use it for baking or to sweeten tisanes; use the stems to grill fruit kebabs; float a few flowers in a glass of indifferent bubbly; sprinkle on goats' cheese, with which it has a curious affinity, or try these lavender biscotti to waken some of the 180 fragrance notes that make up this evocative fragrance.

Melt and cool 2 tablespoons unsalted butter, add 225g sugar, then two beaten eggs plus two extra whites. Sift in 450g plain flour, a teaspoon of baking powder and a pinch of salt. Add a tablespoon of lavender buds and mix together for a stiff dough. Roll into four logs and place on an oiled tray, then bake for 15 minutes at 170C/325F.

When cool, cut into diagonal slices an inch thick and place on two oiled trays. Bake for a further 45 minutes at 130C/275F. Leave to cool. Alternatively, try flavouring these biscotti with fennel seeds and pistachios, or chopped rosemary with walnuts.

18th

I have bumblebees living under my floorboards with access from the ventilation bricks in my bay windows. Of the 24 different species that live in this country, I wonder which sort they are. They're all under threat because there are far fewer flowers in the countryside to provide bees with the pollen and nectar they need to survive. Bumblebees, of all pollinators, are vital to farmers and gardeners, because their furry coats keep them warm during cold days when others won't venture out, so all early crops, especially fruit, need these fat, friendly bombers.

As a nation, our gardens cover more than a million acres and could be the bumblebees' lifeline, providing bee-friendly plants that flower early in the season, like pulmonaria, aubretia, English bluebells, primroses, pussy willow, single crocus and white deadnettle, which will feed all pollinators on sunny spring days.

I'm tempted to set up a hive of honeybees at the bottom of the garden in among the protein-rich clover. Recently, one of the local allotmenteers applied to keep some on her plot. The council contacted all the householders whose gardens back onto the allotments. Just one protested, so the whole plan had to be dropped. I'll wait till my grandchildren are a little older and then talk to the local beekeeping association to find a mentor to hold my hand through the first year. In the meantime, I must try to remember always to plant those flowers that'll help all those useful creatures: colourful, simple, single, native, fragrant flowers in a warm sunny sheltered spot. Bees need our flowers for nectar and pollen, adding variety to a diet suffering from barren sprayed verges and industrial orchards, with a surplus of oilseed rape.

A herb garden would definitely be the bees' knees. Herbs and honeybees have a historical affinity, both have manifold medicinal and culinary uses, in reality and folklore, right up to the present day. Watch them as they luxuriate on angelica, allium and fennel heads, work their way through the sage, rosemary and marjoram flowers, and then busy themselves buzzing among the mints. I was always told never to let herbs flower, it exhausts their fragrance, but it's a price I'm prepared to pay.

Up until the 18th century, honey was the main sweetener in cooking: sugar replaces half its weight in honey, bringing its own special flavour to cakes and fruit puds. Try topping good vanilla ice cream with cubed comb honey; use honey to glaze meat and ham; melt a spoonful in marinades for game and poultry mixed with lemon, ginger and spices; brush it on roast veg with herbs; use it in dressings with mustard and olive oil and to sweeten custards infused with lavender and rosemary flowers.

Drizzle warm honey on figs stuffed with ricotta and pared lemon peel; stuff baked apples with dates, honey and chopped hazelnuts; sweeten spiced plums and poached pears, and deaden a winter cough with hot lemon, turmeric and honey.

22nd

To London, to the Garden Museum in Lambeth to celebrate the publication of Joy Larkcom's autobiography – *Just Vegetating* – and a talk by Joy, over from her 'retirement home' in Ireland. When, last year, the editorial edict went out to find someone you really admire to write about to celebrate the *Sunday Telegraph*'s 50th birthday, I had no hesitation in bagging Joy Larkcom. Without doubt, she has had more effect on the way we grow and eat salads and vegetables than all the well-feted celebrity chefs that supermarkets endorse. So, forgive me Joy, you've never blown your own trumpet – let me redress the balance, and indulge in a little hero worship.

Described as the original hunter-gatherer, Joy studied horticulture at Wye, and her academic background has encouraged her to dig deep. She writes about what she knows, and what she has grown. When we spoke, she was just back from a visit to Australia and has not lost any of her wanderlust, describing how she and her young family set off in a caravan for their Grand Vegetable Tour in 1976, travelling from Holland to Hungary, studying vegetable culture and bringing back valuable heritage seeds. She discovered purslanes, endives and a whole range of chicories, and can be held responsible for that scattering of rocket leaves on every dish in every restaurant.

She also promoted the intensive method of salad cultivation known as cut-and-come-again, something packet salad producers and anyone with a small garden will thank her for. Since then she has travelled the world, lured by tempting and unknown plants, especially oriental vegetables (which can be sown from seed now for autumn salads).

Under her influence, the British Salad finally regenerated from a soggy tomato with limp lettuce leaves bathed in a vinegary pink beetroot jus to one I documented in a small book Joy generously helped me with in 1998: 'a palette of flavours, textures and colours from fernlike dill to crisp pak choi, to lemony buckler-leaved sorrel and bitter chicory; augmented with handfuls of rocket, basil and garlic chives from the herb garden; and young chard leaves, asparagus tips and blanched runner beans from the veg plot, decorated with nasturtium and borage flowers'. Among the verbiage, you can spot the difference, and that's thanks to Joy.

We've known each other vaguely for years. In Suffolk she was Salad Queen to my Chicken Woman, and having both left to downsize by the sea, me to coastal Kent and Joy to Southern Ireland – I asked if she regretted the move. Absolutely not. Although her new garden is just half an acre, she says the older she gets, the bigger it seems. She had planned it to be low-maintenance, but has totally failed. The mild climate means things grow too fast, and the salty winds blacken the plants. Like me, Joy has planted a lot of fruit, including an inspirational apple allée, much of which is lost to the birds.

Joy and her husband – the indefatigable Don Pollard, who she says 'enables me to carry on and only occasionally asks if I ever intend to stop' – are pleased with their new life, but like us all, just wish they had more time and energy. She threatens *Just Vegetating* will be her last book. Put it next on your reading list.

I often think of Joy as I harvest my lunch from my tiny vegetable garden, snipping buckler-leaved sorrel, tarragon sprigs, cos lettuce leaves and chive flowers to eat with halved hard-boiled eggs and a lemony dressing. Or as I use a new favourite salad leaf – close-planted pea-shoots, eaten with garden peas, snipped bacon and a chopped mint vinaigrette – one of our favourite meals of the year. For vegetarians we substitute roast pine nuts or pumpkin seeds.

26th
I picked my first blackberry today. It was a bit sour, but there'll be plenty more, the season seems to go on till the first frost, after which time the berries are said to have been touched by the devil. I'm longing to show Ludo Prospect Field, to examine the puddles together, blow dandelion clocks, pick up stones and run on the rabbit-cropped grass – it'll be nice for him to be able to race about untrammelled. We'll hop and skip and watch the trains, and then after a picnic of juice and biscuits on one of the benches, we'll walk back. It'll be nice to experience a second childhood with such a sweet companion.

27th
Another walk, along the coast, with friends this time, showing off the variety of plants that grow on the beach. Acid-yellow horned poppies, purple vetch and sea kale, pink, white and red valerian and blue-mauve echiums (viper's bugloss), all growing almost down to the pebbled water's edge, beside the groins and sea defences. Perhaps we don't have miles of golden sand, but this is a seaside world full of insects, birds and colour.

A good friend of mine lives right on the beach. As a gardener she has the best of both worlds. Her front garden is a sheltered green oasis leading down steps to her wooden house, and beyond, she has her own strip of beach and some of the most spectacular views along the north Kent coast. Of course, seaside gardening is not the easiest terrain: howling north-easterly gales, salt-laden air, shallow dry soil and public access across your eye line will try your patience, but the seascape is the backdrop to your life, and every day is a holiday.

To take advantage of spectacular sunsets, summer meals are eaten along the sea side on sun-bleached wooden decking, hung with homemade bunting, and surrounded by pink, white and red valerian, magenta lychnis, blue sea holly, fennel, hebes, sea peas and toadflax, scented with lavender, rosemary, santolina and purple sage – good doers that all love the site, because there's little point in growing plants that don't repay your hospitality – all protected by grey-leaved buckthorn and strategically placed pebbles and driftwood.

29th

I've noticed a lot of Whitstable people are flamboyantly talented, none more so than Peggy Eagle who brings her puddings to the farmers' market every Saturday. I try not to look as I pass her stall – I can resist everything except temptation in the pudding department – but with her maxim 'occasional indulgence is good for the spirit' ringing in my ears, I deceive myself that a seasonal fruit-based pudding is somehow less wicked, and confess to having succumbed to her plums with star anise and black pepper, her cream pots with crab apple and rosehip reduction, and her avocado and lime cheesecake.

Time to harvest currants from the fruit cage, so I asked Peggy to practise her alchemy on those tart little jewels: translucent white currants, the zingy reds and musky blackcurrants and turn them into irresistible puds. She suggested a blackcurrant clafoutis: sweating the fruit with sugar in a heavy pan, then covering with a vanilla-flavoured eggy batter and cooking in a moderate oven till set. Then a modern summer pudding of stacked juice-soaked brioche rounds in between layers of black- and redcurrant compote, set inside a washed and oiled tin (ex-baked bean tins make good formers) in the fridge, then eased out and decorated with redcurrants. And finally, pretty white currants floating in a mouth-watering gooseberry and elderflower jelly, set with agar. And I had to try them all . . .

30th

At the end of July, Whitstable holds its annual Oyster Festival – a wild affair, reinventing the fishermen's Norman feast that offers thanksgiving for their harvest and survival from the sea. July is one of the months (without an 'r') that augurs the closed season, so not the best of times to sample native oysters. If visitors, including this year, Prince Charles and the Duchess of Cornwall, celebrate the festival with a half dozen, they will be imported pacific oysters. Presumably, it's a period of the year when the fishermen had time to relax and hold a festival, with its time-honoured church blessing, jolly floats, drunken tourists and 'grotters' made of shells and sand, lit by candles and built by families

on the beach. Native oysters love the estuarine waters here as they mix with the incoming tidal seawater. Seamus Heaney described their taste on the tongue as 'a filling estuary, hung with starlight'.

I can take or leave oysters. They are best opened to order and eaten straight on a bed of crushed ice at Wheelers, a little pink restaurant and shop counter in the High Street. Other eateries serve them with a dash of Tabasco, a squeeze of lemon juice or vinegar with chopped shallots; on toast with anchovies and cream, grilled with parmesan, or coated in Guinness batter.

We are really spoiled here with a huge range of excellent restaurants, but their popularity makes it difficult to eat out spontaneously without booking weeks ahead. Be warned, if you're planning a visit during Festival Week, I've even queued for over an hour for fish and chips.

181

AUG*ust*

Haymaking

Apricots & Greengages

Porch Succulents

Beach Hut Birthdays

Wedding Anniversaries

Tomatoes, Peppers & Aubergines

Henhouses

2nd

Whitstable is hotting up. With the Oyster Festival over, family holidaymakers and day-trippers are pouring in. It's quicker to walk than drive into town, especially over the weekends. I love the fact that people want to come here, but selfishly don't really want to be with them, so living on the edge of town comes into its own. The coast along West Beach and Seasalter, bereft of facilities and attractions and a brisk promenade from the main drag, is virtually empty. On pleasant days, to tell the truth, I'd rather relax in the garden, with my familiars – cat and hens around me.

Relax with a jug of iced homemade cordial – blackcurrant, or raspberry are best – (boil the fruit till soft, mash and re-boil with sugar to taste, place in a jelly bag to strain, then mix a pint of strained juice sweetened to 1lb caster sugar) delicious slaked with sparkling dry white wine, as is any sliced fruit marinated in alcohol: strawberries in champagne, gooseberries in Sauternes or white currants in hock.

There's art to relaxing in a garden you care for. How to switch off and ignore that weed, or those wilting plants, that clash of colours or unfortunate partnership, and allow your mind to drift. I know as I sit and write in the meadow, that sooner or later, the long grass, now blond, dry and lovely, will need to be cut. In my efforts to make the gardening year less arduous, this is an annual task I leave to others, along with major hedge cutting (I'm happy to trim). Our first haymaking was carried out by a group from Appleseed, a now sadly defunct Kent Enterprise Trust initiative that supported young people overcome challenges through horticultural training, who helped me subdue the wilderness of my new garden in the spring.

Enter Project Manager Becky Richards, Community Gardener James Thorn and enthusiastic trainees carrying rakes and scythes. We were taught to stand correctly, stomachs in, knees bent, backs straight, before swinging the scythes in an arc, sweeping the grass and everything else in its way. I soon learnt, scything is not a 'one lesson' skill, it requires stamina and practice, so it's a raker's life for me. With wooden hay rakes, we built a satisfying haystack under the oak tree to slowly compost, leaving a bare patch that I can replant with English bluebells as part of next year's spring woodland garden. I think, sadly, next year someone will have to strim the grass.

The best meadows in a domestic setting are at Great Dixter, where they manage their highly ornamental fields to maximize diversity of plant, insect and birdlife, and in particular to encourage varieties of wild orchids. Their meadows are cut late with a power scythe to allow seed to ripen, then strewn to encourage seed distribution. The hay is collected and the grass cut right down to the ground. A few areas are left uncut to provide cover for wildlife – we should all try and leave part of our gardens unkempt over winter.

In my orchard area, I have planted drifts of bulbs and rectangles of wildflowers. I have sown patches of blue flax (from the health food shop), which should re-seed, white and yellow ox-eye daisies and Californian and opium poppies, but primarily native grasses that sway in the breeze and catch the late afternoon sun.

4th

Have been busy painting my porch, the outside on sunny days, and on cooler days inside, because it's like a furnace in that tiny vestibule with the sun beating down. The floor is tiled, some respite perhaps, with old quarry tiles, and much of the glass is original. I have been collecting ornate wirework shelf units from car-boot sales, to display my rapidly increasing collection of tender succulents.

While I feel I can boast modest success growing plants in the garden, I seem to be the kiss of death to indoor plants. I always end up mistreating those desiccated sprigs – maybe it's their total reliance on me that I resent. Now, happy in their new home, the sole survivors of a once flourishing conservatory, my succulents are my horticultural guilty pleasure.

As a genus, succulents are a complicated family, but many are easy to grow in specific locations. Both tender glasshouse and hardy garden varieties are strangely addictive. Apart from shelves of tender echeverias, agaves and crassulas, I also admit to a penchant for the hardier sempervivums and sedums that grow anywhere outside: in pans, troughs or, as I am trying, in beds, like living Persian carpets. I have bedded them out into soil, lightened with sacks of horticultural grit and bound with retrieved barleycorn twist edging tiles, so, there on either side of my front door, my secret passion will be on display, for all to see.

My first plants came from generous friend and intrepid gardener at the Abbey in Eye, Kate Campbell. She, in turn, amassed her magnificent collection from friends all over the world, furtively pocketing little pieces and growing them on in her two impressive greenhouses, shaded in summer with whitened panes. Succulents are accommodating plants, easy to propagate by plucking offsets, to pot on or hand out to other collectors. In my turn, I have shared my plants with roof gardeners, kitchen windowsill propagators and other succulent geeks.

With flowers like riotous fireworks in bright orange, yellow and scarlet, that seem to appear overnight on long shooting stems, the variation in leaf colour and texture is equally mind-blowing. From powdery blue to downy grey, near black to floury white, some have frilly pink-edged petticoats or sculptured glaucous green rosettes, reflecting their exotic South American roots.

Adapted to withstand a wide range of temperatures and conditions, these plants are monocarpic with rosettes that die after flowering, throwing out little 'chicks' that root and spread. Their fleshy stems and leaves act as water storage containers to minimize evaporation, which is why mine survive despite my periodic neglect. They spend part of their summer holidays outside, enjoying the fresh air, and up until three winters ago, in milder times, some echeverias could even be considered hardy.

Have a go! Clothe the roof of a shed, fill an old stone sink, pop them in any old crevice and give in to the pleasures of growing Crassulaceae.

5th

Meanwhile in the main garden, work goes on apace creating a seating and eating area. When I was planning my previous garden thirty-odd years ago, I can't remember dedicating such a large portion to this purpose – nearly a third of my new plot has been set aside – perhaps in the meantime, we've become a nation of al fresco diners, maybe the weather really is warmer, or more likely I spend more time sitting down.

When designing a garden, I start from the house and look outwards, not just to frame the view in the distance, but to concentrate on the bit I use the most. My French windows are like the frame to a portrait of my garden, and look through to a small decked courtyard in the shelter of this house, bound to one side by the weatherboarded garage and to the other by the washroom extension, coloured to echo the house. The roof slates and stock bricks have determined my palette of purply-grey and sandy yellow, and old slate larder shelves house galvanized containers. The two yellow brick paths that lead off to the orchard were laid by me, using bricks rescued from the skip, and bonded with Dansand, an organic silica/sand mixture, supposed to inhibit weed growth – but sadly not my weeds, so bang goes hope of spending less time on hands and knees, wielding a kitchen knife.

The small picnic lawn for Ludo to take his first steps, easily cut with my whirring vintage cylinder mower – lubricated regularly with WD-40 and sharpened before each mow with my tiny Istor sharpener (from niwaki. com) – is easy to manage, so no more futile attempts to pull-start petrol mowers. With two tiny vegetable beds to my left and a working area on the right, I feel I have everything to hand, making a real stab at low-maintenance gardening with barely a conifer or decorative mulch in sight.

I prefer to work potting and planting standing, so along the hedge, Martin, who makes beach huts, is building a workbench from timber that somehow made its way in the removal vans from Suffolk. Built sturdily to take my small Beehive outdoor oven, an ancient low stone sink, a cedar potting tray, and anything else that needs to be kept away from small hands, we are also planning a low round table for plants, built from decking offcuts that will double up as extra seating.

Covered in large beach pebbles (I had hoped to continue the seaside theme and carpet this bit with cockle shells from the harbour, but the smell put me off; maybe I could use them on the path to the chicken run so the extra calcium would strengthen the hens' eggshells), this area – fenced off from the rest of the garden with a tall bay hedge and espaliered apple trees – is the heart of the garden. It's close to the kitchen and occasionally shady – not everyone welcomes the sun – with plenty of comfortable Lloyd Loom chairs with fat cushions.

When the meal is over we usually head to the old metal swinging seat rusting slowly away in the long grass in the orchard. On its last legs (good to know I could get a replacement from The Idler), Max has used his welding skills to good effect, because this heirloom is a must for fractious babies and those who spend important time in the garden just dreaming. I plan to surround this space with more roses: 'Munstead Wood', I think, and maybe ramblers like 'Veichenblau', 'Violette' or 'Amadis'.

192

The flavour of roses in cooking is difficult to get right. Frances Bissell recommends the deep pink to dark red spectrum from old-fashioned Rosa officinalis, R. gallica and R. centifolia. Many rose-tinted jellies, macarons and syrups taste cloying, but if you have a rosy fragrance you really love, try making your own rose petal syrup by boiling 400ml water, then pour over 50g sweet-smelling petals, and leave to diffuse for several hours. Gently dissolve the sugar in the mixture on a low heat, cool, strain and bottle. Try this syrup with baked peaches or figs, or in a simple fruit salad with sliced apricots and nectarines. On uneventful days, I also enjoy crystallizing flower petals (and whole primroses and pansies) by painting them with egg white on a fine paintbrush, dredging them with caster sugar and leaving them to dry on parchment. I have a rather dusty primrose on a shelf that must be at least three years old.

12th

The anniversary of Jacques and Saskia's wedding in Suffolk. My mother always had ambitions for her rebellious daughter to attend the Constance Spry School of Flower Arranging – a career path I have never regretted declining – until a few years ago, when my son and his lovely Saskia decided to get married. I longed to stage the wedding at my garden, but the guest list soon outgrew the venue, and sensibly they agreed to have a garden wedding, but at her Aunt Mossy's, with homemade decorations, home-cooked food – and flowers home-grown by me.

Luckily, I hedged my bets and gave packets of seeds to all my gardening friends, because growing conditions that summer were not ideal. We bit our nails as drought followed late frosts and torrential rain, but come the day, we mustered bunches of cerise cosmos, wavy *Verbena bonariensis*, spiky lavender, Shasta daisies, cornflowers and coneflowers, Michaelmas daisies, rudbeckia, green and magenta zinnias and a fabulous range of sunflowers from Seeds of Italy.

The evening before, the wedding flowers were arranged loosely in airy bunches and displayed in dozens of vintage cut-glass vases, some of definitely dubious taste, collected over months of enjoyable car-booting and charity shop trawls. My best friend from school, Jane, and I made chicken-wire balls to fit in each vase, added a liberal dash of Chrysal Clear cut-flower food – Constance wouldn't have been impressed – and created arrangements for each table. The bride's – a stylish fluted vaseful of rudbeckia, spiky wheat and small cream moonshine sunflowers (to match her satin brocade thirties' dress) was delicate and beautiful, like the bride herself; while my table sported verbena and green zinnia 'Purple Prince' and 'Envy' to complement my LK Bennett suede shoes and sixties' Nottingham lace dress that cost £10 from the RSPCA shop.

The marquee was decorated with garlands of faux sunflowers from W&M Smith (an Aladdin's cave for wedding accessories), metres of bunting sewn by Jacques (we knew that sewing machine proficiency badge from primary school would come in useful), and huge baskets of cream, rust and maroon sunflowers – which carried on flowering till October. We made vintage fabric pennants in small flowerpots to differentiate the tables, lit with long-lasting tealights in Kilner jars, and outside, the trees were hung with Chinese paper lanterns and strings of multi-coloured lights. As the night grew distinctly chilly, we warmed ourselves round huge fire buckets and sat on straw bales covered with woolly rugs and Indian bedspreads.

Guests with culinary pedigrees were asked to bring puddings. Using up our surfeit of apricots, we made little biscuit-based tarts in tin trays. Topping each one with a half a stoned apricot face down with a ball of marzipan in place of the stone, we poured over a custard mixture of 280ml single cream, 3 egg yolks and 85g vanilla sugar per tray. The trays were then baked in the oven till the custard set, and served cold with a raspberry sauce.

Apricots are the coming fruit. With warmer springs and longer summers, they are now even grown commercially here. Peach leaf curl is a thing of the past with new disease-and frost-resistant varieties, like 'Tomcot' and 'Flavourcot', so there's nothing to stop us growing these luxuries. I'd been harvesting abundant apricots for the past seven years in Suffolk. Every summer, we'd pickle, bottle and gorge ourselves, best of all we finish a special meal like they do in Italy: at some stage towards the end of the meal, someone needs the presence of mind to chop whichever fruit is in season, to pop them into glass dishes and top up with dessert or sparkling wine. As the evening wears on, both fruit and alcohol can be topped up . . .

A fairytale wedding, just a lovely memory now. The Humanist ceremony, with close friends and family, was almost unbearably moving, as we all felt the loss of both the bride and groom's fathers. Jean-François and Chris would have loved this party, standing at the back, ciggies and drinks in hand, taking pride in their children.

19th

Drinks on the beach. I totter over the groins and pebbly path along Seasalter beach in party clothes, clasping bottles and homemade nibbles. As the deck comes into focus, I notice an unexpected crowd of people, who all shout 'Happy Birthday' as we appear. A surprise party! Horrors! I'm not good at my birthday – it's not that I bemoan the passing of the years, and I love making other people's birthdays happy, I just never really enjoy myself. But what started as one of my least favourite celebrations, ended – after many toasts – as a joyous evening with new friends. I really do feel at home here in Whitstable.

20th

A garden without livestock is a dull and dreary place. I've missed the drama and movement poultry brings to a garden, and I love my glorious new henhouse in shades of sunny yellow. Where else would I go to have my new henhouse made than Jacques? Between us we had fun and came up with a beach hut-inspired design, featuring a shingle roof and an innovative sliding nestbox drawer for easy access to all those tasty eggs.

The whole edifice is lined with ply, with siliconed joints to avoid creating similarly comfortable accommodation for parasitic mites. I asked for the house to be put on legs, to discourage rats and other burrowing pests, to create a purpose-built dust bath underneath, and to encourage regular cleaning habits in this slovenly hen-wife.

The run is more of a problem. Foxes are a common sight here (as they are throughout urban Britain); three doors down there is derelict garden, ideal habitat, backing on to the allotments and the railway line. My only hope is that these are nocturnal country foxes with a healthy dislike of humans, distracted by the hundreds of rabbits on Prospect Field and the railway embankment, still wild enough to eschew human company, and not urbanized vermin that feed on rubbish and cavort in gardens at any time of the day or night.

We've built a stockade covered run on the east side of the garden, so the hens get the afternoon sun, the shelter of an ancient birch and a solid fence behind them. Hens need shade and shelter from the elements, as well as safety from predators. I've fenced the run with 2-metre chestnut posts – tall enough to take a fruit netting roof (there is nothing worse than not being able to stand up straight in your run) and bird-proof wire, bringing it out into a protective apron, pegged down to prevent digging intruders. Gone are the carefree Suffolk days, when for thirty years, I never saw or heard a fox, dead or alive, thanks to local gamekeepers. I'm living in the real world that confronts most henkeepers, with constant worry about my flock's wellbeing.

Generally, I don't recommend that those with a newly planted garden embark on keeping free-range birds, but I'm hoping to outwit mine with years of experience gardening with hens. First, I'll contain them within the orchard and bosky areas – ideal territory, because chickens are descended from jungle fowl and like a bosky spot, and everything I plant will have its roots protected from scratching feet by pebbles and its delicate shoots from pecking beaks by cloches and nets. My vegetable beds and seating area will be out of bounds, so I can grow salads un-nibbled and we can relax in a chicken poo-free environment. (Needless to say, this resolution didn't last long . . .)

22nd

Birthday lunch down at the Beach Hut. Unpromising start with windy drizzle, but we pack rugs and umbrellas instead of swimming gear and towels and head off with a basket of food and drink to open up the hut. Max builds windbreaks and a barbecue in their lee, keeping the rain off the fire with an umbrella, the doors are spread wide to act as further shelter and we open bottles early and prepare to eat. Ludo will love playing house by the sea, though at times we have been more like the characters inside a Swiss weather house, as we pop in and out to escape the showers.

Outdoor meals have developed a pattern: something sausagey or fishy on the fire, delicious bread from local baker – Tobias Schwenn; huge platters of salad and then a party pud. A few months ago I found a mammoth moulded glass plate at the car-boot. Someone had painted the underside gold. Already chipping, it wasn't hard to clean off with brush cleaner, and now it's a really useful dish.

There is nothing as redolent of summer as the smell of sun-ripened, misshapen home-grown tomatoes, aubergines and peppers. Grill a few sliced aubergines and long red peppers with a little olive oil and salt (save the pan juice to add to the dressing). Arrange like petals on a large round dish. Slice beefheart tomatoes (fluted 'Costoluto Genovese' or rich 'Brandy Wine' are good), add quartered purple plums and stripy 'Tigarella', halved red and yellow cherries and scatter with tiny currant tomatoes. Cover with crumbled mild feta – good feta should taste of more than salt – and add this dressing.

I have tried to grow late summer basil in the ground, much to the delight of the slugs, but inevitably end up growing plants in pots. At the end of each pot of basil, I make tiny amounts of pesto, using up old leaves and stalks with pine nuts, pumpkin seeds, loads of garlic, all pounded with a little lemon juice and lots of olive oil, just enough to make a rich dressing for centre-stage salads.

I often feel our summer aren't long enough to grow many vegetables to their full potential. The old solution was to set the seed really early, and windowsills would be crammed with leggy seedlings, craning for sunlight too soon to move them out. The modern way is to grow varieties bred in cooler climes that germinate well in cold conditions, set seed earlier and are productive over a longer period. Ben and Kate Gabel from The Real Seed Catalogue have come up with a list of varieties, including 'Latah', 'Legend Bush', 'Grushovka' and 'Urbikany' tomatoes, 'Sweet Chocolate', 'Lipstick' and 'Purple Beauty' peppers and 'Ronde de Valence' and 'De Barbentane' aubergines, perfect for our variable climate. And they give instructions how to save your own seed.

29th

After a couple of weeks of computer hell, am now sitting in front of a toweringly menacing iMac. I'm sure like most owners, I will get to love it, but at the moment the changeover from ancient PC is fraught. In the hiatus, I lost all my history, and worse my addresses. They were recovered eventually. My inability to cope with technology is worrying. My small success with the Mac – yes, it does all makes sense, encouraged me to rush and buy a smartphone. Disaster – my shaky hands can't tap in a phone number, the digits appear in multiples, so it's back to the ancient mobile, which I use so infrequently that I usually have to ask strangers on trains how it works.

30th

With another significant birthday passed and my mother's experience still horrifically fresh in my mind, thoughts occasionally drift to my own future. Genetics influence a third of our health apparently, so I look back with optimism to my grandmother who lived at home, drove a Sunbeam Rapier and played bridge well into her nineties. Her twin daughters though, both suffered from dementia.

They're a long-lived bunch, the women in my family, but no one wants to live longer if they're going to be ill. We can help ourselves. I believe, like Virginia Woolf, 'One cannot think well, love well, sleep well, if one hasn't dined well.' What we eat is who we are, and most of us are lucky enough to have the luxury of choice. A menu of nuts, eggs, seeds, fish, fruit and veg – home-grown if possible, with occasional forays into the world of junk food, and the hope to eat most in the company of others, is the ideal.

Good diet, regular exercise, an active brain with the knowledge that optimistic people live longer, this is the litany for a lifestyle to keep us independently hale and hearty, hopefully.

SEPT*ember*

Pears

Indian Summer

Car Boots

Cobnuts

Damsons, Plums & Gages

Feathers & Fennel

Zinnias

1ˢᵗ

Indian Summer! Quite the most evocative phrase in the meteorologist's lexicon. It's a bounteous extension and we've been blessed with a longer ripening harvest. I make more effective resolutions at this time of the year, to write more frequently, to walk more and to drink less, to travel and visit more. Maybe it's all down to this low light that shows the autumnal colours so effectively and increases mellow endorphins.

2ⁿᵈ

My usual circuit, and there's a bonanza crop of plums, damsons, bullace, mirabelles, sloes and cherry plums ready to harvest. All growing along Prospect Field, West Beach and the golf course: sports, crosses and remnants of the old orchards that were farmed right down to the sea. I notice all the east-facing trees are barren, their off-white early blossom probably decimated by frost and morning sunbeams, but the rest are groaning with fruit.

I pick a bagful, mixed and colourful and bring them home to cook with a few rhubarb stalks I took from the fruit bed because they were shading the strawberry runners. The result is a passable jam, sweet and sharp in a rich ruby red, delicious eaten with toasted brioche sprinkled with cinnamon sugar.

The best pudding of the year. Plums stewed with vanilla and muscovado sugar, topped with a layer of sliced brioche, sprinkled with roast hazelnut oil and toasted under the grill. Roast hazelnut oil is available from cobnutoil.co.uk.

Every year I try and categorize the drupes, which is which, but I'm still none the wiser. All the wild ones seem to be versions of *Prunus insititia,* but the difference between bullace and damson seems to be down to the shape of the fruit and texture of the stone, rather than colour or taste (bullace are round with smooth stones and damsons are oval with rough). All need lots of sugar to be made palatable and are enhanced with vanilla, but some varieties like damson 'Merryweather' and the shepherd's bullace are sweet enough to eat from the tree. All plum-like fruits have an affinity with almonds, so frangipane tarts and clafoutis made with ground almonds are just the ticket.

Scatter a buttered and sugar-dusted dish with pitted damsons or bullace. Blend together 100g ground almonds with 100g caster sugar and 2 eggs plus 3 yolks. Add 250ml double cream and some good vanilla essence. Bake in an oven (350F/170c) for 20 minutes till brown. Dust with cinnamon sugar and slivered almonds and serve warm. Also delicious with stoned cherries or gooseberries.

8th

An early start at the car-boot sale, helping a friend sell her surplus clothes, jewellery, shoes and odds and ends. Good space at the local community centre, undercover, but it's the first of the year with little publicity, so not great sales. Still, good dry run, as we all have to sell stuff each time we move, whether downsizing or upsizing. Go online to find car-boot sales near you, then pay them a visit, asking stallholders what the form is. Beware, as you arrive, before your stuff leaves the boot, dealers will pounce on your stock. Be tough with them or they'll take advantage; and

don't leave it too late in the season or you'll have to put up with the vagaries of the autumnal weather. Take a stall with a friend, for moral support and an extra hand – it's hard work lugging boxes.

A garage sale in your own backyard is the easiest option, best before you move, then you aren't paying to transport unwanted items, but often, it isn't until you actually move into your new home that you realize just how many of your belongings are surplus to your needs. Prices have to be v. low, but the idea is to shift stock. There are knacks to selling: eye contact, always look busy – never just sit, move your stock around and above all, keep a sense of humour with your potential buyers.

Alternatively, try eBay, free local selling sites, second-hand and charity shops. Persuade your children, friends and family to take anything they want, and sell to those buying your house. I was lucky to have a shop at my previous house. I sold household stuff from the garage, clothes in our vintage clothing department and everything else to others as Christmas presents, probably reducing my property by half. There's nothing to stop you doing the same thing yourself, email your friends, have a party and leave your neighbourhood with a bang.

I found that divesting myself of my chattels was a liberating experience. When taking stock, the amount of stuff we accumulate can be overwhelming, especially when it

215

comes to packing. Better to find a new home for it all, and take care, once ensconced in your new home, not to start the whole process again, especially as car-boot sales can become addictive.

10th

How the weather has changed! So much for our Indian summer. Back home to an afternoon working in the garden full of feathers and cobwebs. And my poor hens are out with barely a feather between them. All birds moult in autumn, even garden birds keep a low profile as they change gear. Tidying, potting, snipping, with my birds scarifying after me, I can see they have stopped moulting and are like partial porcupines as the feathers grow back through quills filled with blood. Looking far from their best, and in need of plenty of protein to produce their new autumn finery, a tonic is a good idea, so I'll top up their breakfast with a sprinkling of Poultry Spice and speed their return to snug feathery finery, and offer protein-rich snacks of cheese, nuts and sunflower seeds.

Am still expecting the return of my builder to finish work on the second floor of this house. Have lived too long in a half world of someone else's taste upstairs, though mostly in the dark, asleep. We have planning permission for a large dormer at the top of the stairs, a new bathroom and the division of the front room into two smaller bedrooms.

12th

In the meantime, have decided to complete the front garden. The plants, bought months ago, need to be in the soil. Have cleared the weedy turf, dug in bags of horticultural grit and sharp sand, with a little garden compost, and then covered with a membrane to suppress weeds, which I hope to remove in a few years. I've cut holes in the membrane and planted a mass of *Verbena bonariensis*, fronted by a row of *Iris sibirica* and then a fringe of *Lavandula x intermedia* 'Grosso', and finally a thick layer of gravel. I want the flowers to float, picking up the mauvey-blue tones of the paintwork, and feed the bumblebees that have made nests in the ventilation bricks under the bay windows.

15th

If you're eagle-eyed at this time of the year, you'll spot small caches of green cobnuts in their pale frilly casings at greengrocers or farmers' markets. Grab them while they're in season, crack open their downy shells and nibble them fresh and milky, before they dry and turn into the golden-brown Christmas nuts we know and love.

What is the difference between a hazelnut, a cobnut and a filbert? Just as the cox is a variety of apple, it seems the cobnut is the cultivated form of wild hazel (*Corylus avellana*), and the filbert – named after its inventor Mr Filbert – is a variety of cobnut. Grown since mediaeval times for fencing, staking and wattle and daub construction, I have planted a selection of Kentish cobs under the oak tree at the bottom of my garden, because in the wild, hazels grow well under the canopies of large trees on a wide range of soils, except those that are waterlogged – not a problem in that part of my garden.

I chose 'Kentish Cob' a reliable cropper recommended for domestic use; 'Merveille de Bollwiller', hardy and vigorous with large nuts; 'Butler', a mid to late season cropper easy to de-husk; 'Ennis', a large attractive round nut with superb flavour, and 'Purple Filbert', with large ornamental purple leaves, attractive in the garden, but a poor nut producer – all recommended by the Kentish Cobnut Association.

This year, my reward has been a handful of nuts, lost to squirrels, who left a small pile of husks as a memento of my first year's harvest. Rich in protein, unsaturated fats, cobs are the favourite food of all things furry and feathery, from dormice to nuthatches and woodpeckers (nice if it was these rarities scoffing mine).

Nowadays, most nutteries, or 'plats' as they are known, are to be found here in Kent. Their harvest is sold to greengrocers, and some turned into award-winning oils: cold-pressed virgin and roasted – nectar to be drizzled on vegetables. The rest are turned into smooth nut butter, and the oil – rich in vitamin E – is also used in beauty products.

I asked bespoke caterer Patrick Williams of the Goods Shed in Canterbury, what he would do with golden Kentish cobnuts, as he busied himself with the lunchtime rush. He mentioned meringues, using 100g ground nuts to 8 egg whites, served with blackberries and cream; or using them in chocolate mousse, in cobnut praline, and his assistant George Forster chipped in with a supper of chopped cobs sprinkled over yellow beetroot and melted goat's cheese.

I love them in pesto or in a crumble topping, especially with damsons; chef Tom Kitchen roasts them with pumpkin, Jerusalem artichokes and beetroot; and my friend Penelope Hands uses them in this recipe for cobnut macaroons. Whisk 3 egg whites with a pinch of salt till stiff, then gradually add 80g caster sugar. Fold in 1½ teaspoons

of ground rice and 100g coarsely chopped nuts and drop the mixture into small heaps on sheets of rice paper on two baking trays. Top each biscuit with a nut and bake for 30 minutes at 300F/150C till pale brown, and chewy in the middle.

16th

I have passions for certain colours – blues and purples, limes and oranges, magentas and pale yellow – but at this time of the year, virtually anything goes. The angle, depth and quality of light from the late summer sun eggs on a last chance burst of rainbow profusion, and I just drink it up, storing the hues to last me through till next spring.

There is a plant that hits the spot, the zinnia. Providing I've had the foresight to sow seed in June in rows in the vegetable garden, and remembered to water them occasionally through periods of drought, these are easy plants in sari colours from their Indian homeland – magentas, pinks and greens – echoing the tropical fruits they grow alongside: cordial colours in mango, blackcurrant, lime, raspberry and cherry. *Zinnia* 'Zahara' and 'Elegans', some double, some single, all stunning, and the best of cut flowers. Avoid the dwarf varieties; try 'Envy' or 'Queen Lime' (green), 'Dark Cherry' (deep red) and 'Double Fire' (orange), 'Giant Wine Bouquet' (burgundy), and 'Purple Prince' (magenta). Bring them into the house in bunches, posies and nosegays. These were my mother's favourite flowers, bringing back memories of India where I was born.

221

Great Dixter's gardeners, headed by Fergus Garrett, manage this autumn kaleidoscope of colour with great aplomb, experimenting with texture, scale and glorious colour. Receding walls of planting, with mind-bending combinations of magenta lychnis and mauve verbena, with scarlet guelder berries; backed by purple cardoons and royal blue salvias with lime green *Nicotiana langsdorffii*. And electric blue and pink lace cap hydrangeas with single pink anemones, and clouds of *Thalictrum delavayi* with pink and white *Nicotiana mutabilis*. Simple plants: artfully arranged.

17th

Every year I try and grow Florence fennel and every year I get ferny growth a plenty – and tiny inedible bulbs. To add insult to injury, herb fennel grows here like wildfire, right down to the beach. What we lack, here in the south-east, is rain. Florence likes lots of moisture and a sunny site. Too much sun and not enough water, and the plant will bolt. It takes water to swell the base of the stem that forms the fennel bulb, while the herb will grow in any soil in profusion – whatever the weather. It was the Romans who, by judicious breeding, turned the one into the other, believing it would make them strong and improve their sight. The Greeks called it 'Marathon', investing it with all sorts of magic, including appetite suppression: the first diet food; it was used as a poultice for snakebites; and Charlemagne declared fennel essential in every garden.

Modern research proves fennel to be a virtual pharmacopoeia of useful properties, full of phytonutrients with lots of vitamin C, while the primary component of the seeds' volatile oils, anethole, helps to reduce inflammation. The seeds themselves aid digestion, are used in colic remedies, and you can buy fennel-flavoured toothpaste or chew the seeds to freshen breath. Recent studies have found it helpful for women suffering from PMT.

As a vegetable Florence fennel is even more versatile. Braised or steamed and served with pork or fish it is sublime; deep fried in a light tempura batter it is delicious, or try it sliced with a mandolin with shaved parmesan, or chopped in batons to dip into hummus. My favourite dish is fennel bulbs sliced and caramelized in butter and sugar, then covered in goat's cheese, scattered with fennel seeds and grilled. Fennel loses its flavour soon after it has been cut. Revive it, packed in ice, with a brief stay in the fridge.

I love pickled fennel. Sliced finely, then brined in salty water and steeped in best cider vinegar with a little honey and fennel seeds. Take two cups of fennel. Combine with 3 teaspoons of salt in a bowl of iced water and leave to pickle for at least 4 hours. Mix together ¾ cup of vinegar with ½ cup of water, two tablespoons of honey and bring to the boil. Drain the fennel, rinse in water, pack in sterilized jars and cover with the cooled liquor. Make sure your vegetables are completely submerged (add an extra 2.5cm) under the vinegar solution at all times, or they'll go mouldy. Leave to macerate for a month in a cool place and keep in the fridge once opened.

Use the seeds to make your own spice mix with garden lavender, bay leaves, coriander and cumin seeds, rose petals, nutmeg, cloves and peppercorns. Roast, then grind to steep in olive oil, and dunk chunks of crusty breads. Mix the roasted seeds with black, pink and white peppercorns and salt to make a tasty crust on baked salmon, or combine with chilli in the darkest chocolate.

Umbelliferae are decorative garden plants too, both *Foeniculum vulgare* and its bronze relation will seed themselves and squeeze in all over the border, without elbowing out their companions. Decorative cousins, the noble but inedible *Ferula communis* and *Tigitana* 'Cedric Morris' are worth a space. Even the wildlife appreciates fennel, especially its foliage, beloved by swallowtail caterpillars (and slugs), and the flowers, adored by hoverflies and all sorts of beneficial insects.

18th

This has been a 'mast' year for blackberries – one where the cold winter, warm summer and recent rain have delivered a bumper crop, more than enough for both foragers and wildlife. The downside is that brambles are on the increase, thriving on nutrient-rich soils to the detriment of bluebells and primroses. With my own gargantuan bramble thicket that takes up almost a third of the far end of the garden, we don't have to travel far to blackberry. I pick a large bowl, adding a handful of autumn raspberries and then scurry off to the kitchen to cook my harvest.

I quickly sweat the berries with a little vanilla sugar and water to release the juices, and then we layer it in a buttered pudding basin with slices of brioche. The pudding is weighted with tins of beans then left in the larder for the juices to percolate through the stodge, with luck we'll be able to have a slice with ice cream for tea.

224

The blackberries picked, I decide to spend the autumn dismantling my bramble patch, a task that threatens to overwhelm me, so must be approached as a gradual daily chore. Every afternoon at about three o'clock after a long stint at my desk, I step out, dressed in stout gardening clothes, gloved and hatted, with secateurs in hand, and systematically cut down and chop up every spiky runner, packing them in seven large gravel bags. Some I squash into my green bin, jumping in to compact the contents. I have warned neighbours, that if they hear shouting, to come and rescue me. The brambles take their revenge: my arms and legs are covered in scratches.

Gradually, I recover another 30ft of my garden, discover etiolated shrubs, and right at the back, a gigantic compost heap, years and layers of garden compost, hidden by branches and trees felled by the developers when they sliced the garden in two. The boughs are chopped for the woodpile, and this blessedly unexpected bonus of perfect crumbly compost – the panacea for all my clay soil problems – is carted and dumped all over the garden.

After digging for a while, I excavate a den. A fox den: here in the bosom of my garden, I am harbouring the enemy. It is a marvellous maze of corridors and chambers, easily dug in this friable mixture. Luckily there's no one home. Apparently, the vixen usually digs an extra bolthole when she's planning cubs, so I dismantle the whole demesne and hope she gets the message, and stays in her more desirable residence three doors' down.

227

Cut down to the ground, some of the brambles re-shoot and need digging up, but it's easy in this soil, so over the next few months I think I will have reclaimed my territory, staked my claim and made this part of the garden my own.

21ˢᵗ

Back in the house, the builder is back and the dormer is underway. A scaffolding tent has been built over the roof, and slowly an over-engineered structure of beams is built to house my new bathroom. I had mercifully put aside memories of the ghastliness of building work. The ancient dust that even gets through gaffer tape into every orifice and crevice, with the overwhelming noise and cold – but nothing ventured, nothing gained, and James and his new sidekick Ollie divide the space upstairs into a desirable three bedrooms, two bathrooms plus sewing room . . . while Lulu and I cower downstairs, trying to get on with life.

Lulu has been diagnosed with hyperthyroidism – a condition that seems to be common in elderly cats (she is 15). She eats endlessly, day and night, but is as thin as a rake, is never still and shouts like a demented peacock at a volume that has to be heard to be believed. The cure is a pill a day. Anyone who has ever tried to give a cat a pill will understand the problem. First I try subterfuge – delicious coatings of Marmite, cream cheese or smoked salmon – all licked off the pill; then hiding in sausage, prawns or whatever I'm having for supper – treat eaten, pill spat out; then have to finally resort to wrapping her in a towel and forcible introduction. Some diversionary tactics last for five days, and then it's a change of subterfuge. This is a battle that'll carry on as long as she lives, but there are signs that she is recovering, my lovely Lulu, back to her usual self.

27th

With only the quince left to ripen, time to take stock of the orchard year. A tiny harvest of apricots and greengages, a few cherries that escaped the blackbirds, but plenty of apples and pears. Of course you can't compare apples and pears, but which do you prefer? A crunch on a crisp apple or a feast of buttery pear? Chances are, historically, pears would have been your choice, but nowadays many commercially grown pears – 90 per cent of which are Conference – are sold unripe and unready. Varieties are chosen for their travelling suitability rather than flavour. A glance through an elderly reference book mentions 48 different pears, today only a handful are available to eat, but search for specialist nurseries, like Keepers or Blackmore, and you'll find plenty to grow.

From my window, I can see my venerable Comice struggling after the summer's drought, but laden with russet buttery fruit, and a tiny Kentish Concorde, bowing with pears that promise to be good with chocolate. I wish I'd planted a Beurre Hardy or Beth, both RHS winners with great flavour, but there's still space against the south-facing fence, where it's easier to protect blossom from frost and fruit from the birds. The more varieties grown, the better, as pears need to be cross-pollinated by other varieties. As the fruit ripens on the trees, I'll store those I don't eat or give away somewhere cool, unwrapped, away from my apples.

Members of the rose family, pear trees are now mainly grown on quince rootstock. Left on their own roots, they rocket to the skies, taking their fruit out of reach. I intend to mulch in spring with well-rotted chicken manure. Pears do not need thinning, and while the cordons' side shoots need shortening to three leaves beyond their basal cluster in late summer, bush trees can be lightly pruned when dormant, removing damaged and crossing branches. When your tree has reached its desired height, cut back the leaders by two-thirds.

At this time of the year, I eat a grated pear for breakfast with oatmeal, nuts and yoghurt; pears for lunch sliced with dolcelatte and rocket or beetroot leaves, scattered with walnuts and dressed with grainy mustard vinaigrette; and pears for pudding with homemade custard, sprinkled with brown sugar. I love them poached in port or cassis with lemon peel and bay leaves, or eaten sandwiched with vanilla ice cream and covered in melted dark chocolate. Pears make a delicate grainy sorbet, are boozily delicious preserved in brandy, or dried to last the winter. Eat your best pears raw, poach the next best, and dry the rest.

To dry pears, peel and slice the fruit ¼ inch thick, plunge into a water and lemon juice bath and drain. Add spices: cinnamon, vanilla, star anise or cloves to flavour, then follow dehydrator instructions or oven-dry, by spreading slices on baking trays and bake for 10 to 12 hours at 125F/240C. Store in airtight jars.

30th

Thanks to an email from someone who reads my blog, Lulu and I have a remedy for the pill quandary. There are several cat treats (from naturesmenu.co.uk) that seem to be made from a sort of chewy biltong material – dread to think what. Anyway, this can be moulded into a pellet containing the pill, which is then

eaten with gusto. Occasionally, L manages to spit the pill out, but likes the treat enough for two or three tries and we have to start again from scratch.

OCTober

1ˢᵗ

Bright autumn days, and it's a relief to spend time in the garden, keeping out of the dust. The worst is over, with most of the demolition complete, but family problems have taken the wind out of James's sails, the job is dragging, and we still have a hole in the side of the house. The front bedroom space has been divided into three, as planned. I need two small spare bedrooms and somewhere to sew. Once these rooms are complete, we can isolate them, store all the furniture, clothing and bedding inside them for protection, and I'll move downstairs while my bedroom and bathroom are finished, and the dormer roof is open to the elements.

3ʳᵈ

Sad day, as MG came to retrieve his Brahma and her young cockerel. They went off perkily enough, but the remaining pullets have been traumatised. They were so obviously at the bottom of the pecking order, and now they don't know what to do with themselves. Hens rely on their flock for security, they are vulnerable creatures after all. Try not to increase your flock above half a dozen or so birds, or those at the bottom of the pecking order will have too many picking on them. If you want to keep more, pen them separately with their own house and feeding stations – prime bullying sites – but they can meet in the wide open spaces of your garden.

The rest of the day was spent lifting turf, inserting a layer of grit and planting hundreds of bulbs: *Narcissi* 'Pheasant's Eye' and 'Actaea', camassias, fritillaries, chionodoxia, ornithogalum and alliums in the meadow; scillas, bluebells and cyclamen in the woodland and *Narcissus* 'Thalia' and tulips in pots, while the hens settled, foraged and ate windfall apples.

5th

Apparently, we could all eat a different kind of apple every day for more than five years and still not exhaust the range of varieties we can grow in this country. There are 7500 known apple cultivars worldwide, producing 55 million tonnes per annum, to say nothing of the basketfuls rotting away in all our gardens.

Our quandary is not how to grow apples, but how to store them. Luckily, the most welcome, earliest apples store least well, so eat as many as you can right now. It's the later ripening varieties that are the keepers, thicker skinned and sweeter, they store better, and should be picked straight from the tree (sunny side first), so they are not damaged in transit or fall to the ground. Lift the apple, then twist half a turn; if ready, the fruit should come away in your hand.

Only store your best (leave windfalls for the birds, and damaged fruit for juicing or jamming), in a frost-free cellar, garage or shed with good ventilation and low temperature, and away from mousy visitors. Wrap in batches of each variety, individually in twists of black and white newsprint (coloured ink taints) and place on supermarket cardboard trays, away from other vegetables and fruit, or unwrapped and well-spaced on wooden slatted racks. Check your fruit regularly: one bad apple really can spoil the whole box.

So, what can you do with surplus apples? You could make juice with a fruit press, to freeze in plastic bottles, or stew them lightly with a little lemon juice, sieve and purée, pop

238

into bags and freeze. Both will be welcome during winter months, or you could make jam with blackberries or chutneys with other surplus veg like tomatoes or marrows, or these herb jellies with chopped sage, rosemary or mint.

Chop 1.35g fruit and boil till soft, adding a few sprigs of your chosen herb. Strain overnight through a muslin bag, resisting the temptation to squeeze, or your jelly will go cloudy. Measure the juice and return to the saucepan, adding 350g of sugar to every 570ml of juice. Dissolve the sugar and bring gently to the boil. Add very finely chopped herbs or flowers.

Boil for 10–15 minutes until setting point is reached (test a tiny teaspoon of jelly in a saucer of cold water: if it sets, it's ready). Bottle in pretty jars with Christmas in mind. Windfall apples make the best base, but you could experiment with medlars, quince or crab apples, or currants in summer. The nicest combinations are apple and mint (add a few drops of food colouring if you want your mint jelly to be a traditional green); crab apple and sage; apple and lavender flowers, and redcurrant and rosemary.

6th

A visit to Great Dixter for their Annual Plant Fair. Probably my favourite garden at any time of the year, but especially now, when still full of colour, form and extra interest, because other nurseries have come to show off their wares. Plantsmen from Holland, France and Scandinavia have

241

brought rarities to tempt us, and specialist grass and succulent growers have succeeded in my case. A lovely atmosphere, amateur in the true sense of the word.

10th

There are some fruits you can never quite get enough of, and the only way to satiate your greed is to grow your own. The luscious fig augurs summer's end and is ready to be harvested now. Like olives and citrus, figs are borderline plants in this country, often the season isn't quite long enough for their fruits to ripen. It depends on where you live, the vagaries of each year's weather, and the variety you plant.

Figs don't produce visible flowers, they're inside their pea-sized embryonic fruitlets. The edible fig – *Ficus carica* – contains female and hermaphrodite flowers and is self-fertile. Under glass or in warmer climes, a fig tree fruits three times a year, but here, late spring's fruits will swell, but may or may not have time to ripen before the frosts set in. Later, midsummer fruits won't ripen, so can be removed, apart from the late-summer embryos that develop in leaf axils, and could survive winter with a chance of ripening the following year.

'Brown Turkey' and 'Violetta' are the hardiest and earliest to fruit, but there's a mouth-watering array of more exotic figs that will grow with a little winter warmth under glass. Plant these in wooden or clay pots on wheels and move to frost-free winter lodgings.

Outside, find a sheltered spot in full sun against a south-facing wall, away from where you sit and eat – or you'll need nerves of steel to share your meals with wasps at ripening time. Restrict root growth (or you'll produce leaves at the expense of fruit) by planting pots in the ground, then prune roots annually, or in a root restricting bag, or build a pit with concrete paving slabs and fill the base with plenty of rubble, top up with fertile soil. Water plants well in season – especially after the fruit appears, and net in good time to protect from all-comers. My fig lives in an old rusty dustbin.

Figs never ripen in the fruit bowl, so there's real brinkmanship involved in deciding the optimum moment to pick: that small margin before the fruit is spoiled, eaten by wasps or past its best. A tiny drop of nectar seeps from the fig's eye and the fruit's skin develops a perfect bloom, best to pop it straight into your mouth, right there in the garden.

Halved or slashed in quarters, squeezed from the base, figs open like exotic flowers with velvety skins and pink flesh packed with tiny seeds that pop in your mouth. Cut them fresh in a figgy salad dressed with balsamic vinegar, your best olive oil and a spoonful of honey. Try them soaked in orange water and sliced to top an almond tart; stuff them with ricotta and pistachio nuts; or serve with wafer-thin Parma ham, soft crumbled goat's cheese or dolcelatte with toasted pine nuts.

Second-bests should spend a brief sojourn on a sunny window sill, then straight into a medium oven for 20 minutes, drizzled with honey and a little butter mixed with cinnamon, then served with a dollop of Greek yoghurt and the last of the season's borage flowers.

16th
My mum's birthday. I'm always reminded of her at this time of the year, as I stride by a particular hedge on the corner of Island Wall, full of

perfume coming from a bank of silvery-leaved *Elaeagnus x ebbingei* with tiny tubular cream flowers. She planted a similar hedge outside her flat, against regulations and battled to keep it for ten years (it disappeared within three days of her death.) It's amazing how smells can evoke memories more speedily than any of our other senses. Even the faintest fragrance can bring back a souvenir, and the garden is especially full of possibilities of what scientists call olfactory evoked recall. It seems particular emotions that the smell reminds us of, make our brains reshape the memories through a rose-tinted filter – back to the best of times – nostalgia breeds content – leaving what Proust describes as 'almost impalpable drops of their essence'.

Seasonal flowers, like lilac, wallflowers and sweetpeas, whose perfume haven't been successfully purloined by parfumiers, are particularly evocative and arouse pleasure through memories of a fragrance. Fill your garden with pleasant memories, and breathe deeply.

20th

Vineyards are cropping up everywhere. I spotted a micro-vineyard from the train on allotments near King's Cross station, and community vineyards, where you pay for a share of the vendange either with cash or labour are all the rage. Growing grapes commercially is a long-term venture: a large plot, hefty initial input and four years before you can expect a return on your investment, but

244

the extent to which you get involved reflects the passion you feel for this fruit and its products.

You can grow grapes for juice – where grapes are crushed, pressed, strained, sweetened then bottled; you can grow them for wine – though to tell the truth, I've yet to enjoy a really good glass of airing cupboard Chateau Maison – and it takes 700 grapes to produce a bottle of wine, or you can grow them for the table. I'd plant three table varieties – so they will harvest consecutively – in large pots and grow them inside a south-facing lean-to greenhouse or large porch to protect them from others with a taste for the noble grape.

After harvest, your potted vines are moved outside, leaving space for other tender plants and a cold snap will put pay to any pests and diseases. This is Bob Flowerdew's strategy. He says the vine is a vigorous plant, but with restricted roots, it concentrates on producing fruit rather than leaf. The price you pay for nibbling bunches of grapes is consistent watering, top dressing in spring, a seaweed drench once a month and initial pruning to a standard shape on a single stem with a lollipop head of branches. Subsequent pruning on the top stems to two buds should take place in winter, when the plant is dormant. Thin out your fruit bunches, aiming for quality rather than quantity.

24th
A visit to local arboretum at Mount Ephraim, near Faversham to collect leaves. The trees there were planted

to commemorate family anniversaries (with sixty or so trees donated by friends), and the results are there to marvel at, as the leaves turn, seeds ripen and a dusting of extraordinary fungi pierces the carpet of fallen leaves. A coppice of gum trees, included to celebrate a family member's antipodean roots, is shedding fabulous cinnamon curls, and the trunks of *Betula* 'Snow Queen' shimmer in the distance.

The beauty of trees lies not only in their shape, manner and colouring, but in the texture of their bark, their buds, flowers, berries and seeds, as well as the fleeting turn of autumn colour. I'm obsessed with autumn leaves. A car journey with me in the driving seat during October and November can be a dangerous lurch as I exclaim at each riotous scarlet, each butter yellow and every eye-catching orange, often screeching to a halt to collect a particular goody that I gather up, take home and press between sheets of newspaper under mats in my house.

Some families of trees offer a bonanza of year-round show-stoppers: the rowans, crab apples and acers are generous families, followed in particular by *Parrotia persica* with mottled yellow bark, *Ginkgo biloba* with fan shaped leaves, the tulip tree with large square yellow leaves, and *Cercis canadensis* with heart-shaped leaves in pink and purple. Now's the time to plant *Euonymus* 'Red Cascade' (the spindleberry), *Styrax obassia*, *Eucalyptus pauciflora*, and *Catalpa bignonioides* 'Aurea', and dazzle your neighbours with brilliant colours and a flash of wildlife, as flocks of feasting birds cheer up your garden.

Apparently, leaves fall because during spring and summer they're organs of energy capture, and in autumn a means of eliminating waste, when lack of chlorophyll from reducing sunlight allows the red and yellow carotenoids to show through. The frosts then kill the leaves turning them brown and making them drop. So trees have an annual moult as well.

25th

Like falling leaves, the first few seed catalogues have fluttered through the letterbox. I'll squirrel them away till later, but have cleared out my seedbox, and quickly planted the last few packets and half packets of salad and veg seeds in trays, to get a harvest of micro-greens before the frosts set in.

26th

Nice surprise from one of my hens – a tiny egg. At about 24 weeks old, pink and perky pullets come into lay, so prepare a nestbox in the house, fill it with dried moss from the lawn, or leaves, or straw and pop in a china or rubber broody egg, to give them the right idea. Let's hope it's the first of many.

28th

To London, to Coutts in the Strand, for lunch and to judge the gardeners who have entered into this year's Gardening Against the Odds, the competition set up in Elspeth's memory. But all dressed up with nowhere to go. Last night, a storm tore through southern England, ripping down trees and knocking off chimneys, effectively paralysing the rail network, or at least, this part of the network. No trains from Whitstable or Faversham. So disappointing. Not that it's an easy job, deciding which of the individuals or groups are more worthy of mention. You need the wisdom of Solomon, and it often feels slightly uncomfortable, judging who has the more debilitating odds to garden against.

Should get reports back, and then I'll go and interview the winners. In the past, I've met contestants of such bravery, who have gardened with such stoicism. I've talked to individuals who have overcome personal handicaps to create gardens of inspiration for others, and groups who have turned communal eyesores into oases of peace.

Last year, I met a Bangladeshi lady, who, despite looking after two wheelchair-bound children, had turned a derelict kids' playground into a community vegetable patch. Part of a generation of women who were expected to stay at home and seldom seen, she felt imprisoned in a society where mothers are often blamed for the illnesses of their children. The burden carried in isolation must have been unbearable, but thanks to this project, she has made contact with other gardeners on the estate, and now feels at home.

In 2011, I visited Sherborne Allotments in Southend, and was taken aback by the sound of laughter. Quiet concentration is what I expect from those working on their plots, not giggling and guffaws, and what made it more unusual was that everyone of those gardeners was caring for or suffering from one of the most insidiously dreadful of diseases – Huntington's.

There are only about eight thousand sufferers of HD in this country – thank God – and because it's hereditary, family carers know that 50 per cent are likely to suffer themselves, eventually. Symptoms develop gradually over months and

years, appearing first between the ages of 30 to 50, starting with memory loss, clumsiness and then progressively disabling a person's ability to walk, think, talk and reason. Yet members of the Southend Branch HD group were some of the jolliest people I've ever met, and they have turned a weedy piece of wasteland that used to house prefabs into a haven of tranquillity. Neat boarded beds house all the usual veg and soft fruit, carefully grown, and the allotment offers the group and their carers an escape, a meeting place, to work or rest in the fresh air, for those who in the past rarely left their homes.

I met P, a PhD archaeology graduate, who told me coming to the allotment turned him from a vegetable into someone who grows and eats them. With a wicked sense of gallows humour, much appreciated by the rest of the group, not so long ago he stopped talking. His mum had lost hope of him ever communicating again, but since his visits, he even writes poetry. He loves to work in the deep raised beds, where he grows parsnips – often multi-rooted to everyone's amusement – and garlic, though it can take him hours to plant a single row.

Sufferer J and her carer mum come on the bus once a week, sometimes just to watch, and call this place their bolthole. They agree it is a happy place, even though they all have the disease in common, but it brings them out in the fresh air, sometimes a little too fresh, says M, as she dreams of the warmth of her native Barbados.

253

S likes to be with people. Sitting in the shed, enjoying the company, he loves the mental stimulation of the small sensory garden with herbs, brightly coloured flowers and different textures. His daughter helps, bringing along her nine-month-old daughter. With no cure, not many of those at risk decide to be tested to see if they have the HD gene. But S's little granddaughter is HD-free.

Quartermaster and manager Pat has done wonders locating and persuading donations of building materials, tools and even the impressive shed where members sit in the warm. She comes from a family of nine, five of whom have HD, and although she has heart problems and arthritis, she stoically cooks for those in her care. Understanding the need for sufferers to keep their weight up, she feeds them delicious soups made from allotment produce.

Last, but not least, chairman David is the magician who dreamt up this scheme for his band of co-gardeners. He has overseen the development of this plot into a haven with all mod cons: a disabled loo and paths with wheelchair access. A gentle giant with asthma, he ribs and gently bullies his charges into enjoying themselves – he recently organized their AGM outing dressed up as giant vegetables. His siblings have the disease, and he admits he probably assuages his guilt at being HD-free by dedicating his life to his group, hoping, in his words, that through the allotment, 'he is giving people their lives back'.

My visits often move me to tears. Not of pity, or even anger at their plight, but in admiration of the spirit with which these people garden against the odds. Elspeth would have approved our choices.

31st

Forget All Saints and Souls, spiders and skeletons, witches and bats. Let's admit that trick and treaters are ever so slightly frightening, and then send all that creepy, commercialized tat back over the Atlantic. Instead, let's wassail and celebrate summer's end with the feast of Pomona, goddess of fruits and seeds, with cider, apple dunking, barmbrack fruitcake and toffee apples. Decorate your threshold or porch with harvest fruits, and enjoy these last misty days, before autumn sets in. Heaven knows, we can do with a little light relief at this time of the year.

Take comfort and inspiration from long afternoon walks, and come back with pockets full of conkers, beechnuts and coloured leaves, taking inspiration from medieval England. Look for psychedelic acer, cherry and ginkgo, pick liquidambar, vitis and grey felty aspen leaves. Flat dry them between sheets of newspaper and stick them on to windowpanes so the light shines through like stained glass. Hang up bunches of seed heads and herbs for drying, baskets of nuts, those last few dahlias and pretty pumpkins.

Is it a squash, is it a gourd or is it a pumpkin? The boom in Curcubitae in our kitchen gardens over the past decade has resulted in lots of head-scratching, but in some countries, the same word is used for the whole interbred family. Summer squash have always been popular, and are coming to an end, but recently a wide range of winter squash has joined the party. Gourds are inedible, and pumpkins, apparently, don't count, 'because "pumpkin" is not a botanical term, but a physiological description, applied to any squash that looks like a pumpkin.' Problem solved by Andrea Heistinger, in her erudite tome – *The Manual of Seed Saving* – a book that aims to restore our link with heirloom varieties and offer gardeners the chance to cut out the middleman and propagate our own food plants.

The Real Seed Catalogue is also on a mission to get us to save seeds, and offers a range of vegetable varieties that have time to ripen in our short summer season. They recommend ultra-early 'Boston Squash', orange-fleshed 'Waltham Butternut' and 'Burgess Vine Buttercup', that's easy to peel. If the weather has put pay to your harvest, the shoots, tips and flowers of squash plants are eaten throughout the world: try them steamed or fried or simmered in a little coconut milk.

To tell the truth, the squash family is not my favourite in the kitchen. I love a hearty butternut squash and coconut milk soup warmed with a little harissa, and topped with butter-fried sage leaves to banish the autumn blues; a pumpkin, blue cheese and pine nut risotto to keep me warm till the central heating really has to be turned on, but they're more fun to grow than to eat, unless well-spiced with their watery texture reduced, and squash-based puds are my least favourite way to end a meal.

Desperate to prove myself wrong, I tried oven-roast 'Delica' sprinkled with brown sugar, cinnamon with thick cream and topped with praline almonds. The toppings tasted fabulous, but the texture was cloying and the taste of the squash was bland.

Halloween house-warming with my friend S, who has moved to a flat over her lovely shop. From a three-bedroom terraced house to what only can be described as a bijou apartment in the town's centre. I asked her what the hardest part of her tortuous move had been, as we helped unpack her kitchen, finding hard-pressed shelf room for at least five boxfuls of spices, and she said it was the packing. The memories dredged up as each item was wrapped or discarded were emotionally draining, but twenty bags of clothes and twenty boxes of odds and ends were sent off to charity shops.

NOV*ember*

Gardener's Revenge

Wood & Nuts

Ludo's Naming Ceremony

Bathrooms & Bedrooms

Festive Preparations

Quince, Crabs & Medlars

Drinks for Christmas

1st

Afraid the hole in the roof, the builders' dust, and lots of cuddles with Ludo (toddlers get so many viruses) have finally got the better of me. Have a chest and throat infection that's proving hard to shake off. Am laid low. In an effort to escape the chaos, the cacophony of the wind rattling the scaffolding poles, and the noise of foxes mating, I've moved downstairs, so it's a bedsit life for me – a limiting existence – and I'm looking forward to moving back into my new bedroom, and being persuaded it was all worthwhile.

3rd

In bed, coughing, I've time to remember first seeing this house, making an offer, being refused, moving on to other things, then three months later, hearing it was back on the market. The price was higher than I'd budgeted, but with little competition: mean little bungalows poorly built, mostly between the wars, with tiny gardens. I'd come to realize the potential of this building, and was on tenterhooks till the sale finally came through in mid January. I can remember visiting for the second time at this time of the year, with low light, miserable weather and bizarre decor: my family and friends couldn't see any potential at all.

4th

Feeling slightly better, to cheer myself up, have popped a dozen hyacinth bulbs and lots of 'Paperwhite' narcissi into pots and containers, and left them in the shed in the dark. I'll check every week or so, and when I see green tips poking up above the soil, they can be brought in to flower. To me they are a post-Christmas treat, so I'll leave them in the cold until the decorations are stored, then bring them out into the warm a fortnight before I want them to burst into flower and fill the house with perfume. My supply of leaf mould bagged up last year is ready and friable, like a rich fruitcake mixture, perfect to re-pot the few lilies that have survived the lily beetle. So I'll mix it with a little grit and compost and gently remove the yellow bulbs from last year's pot, searching for fat white beetle grubs to throw to the hens, and pop them into their comfy new beds, ready to flower their socks off in the far-off summer months next year.

5th

Of all the garden's produce: flowers, herbs, veg and fruit, the most under-appreciated is wood. As I sit huddled by my new wood-burner, started with my own kindling, burning a few logs harvested from the garden, I think of all the other uses the wood from this plot fulfils. Apart from occasional heating (I'd need much more land to seriously be self-sufficient in wood), I grow hazel to produce pea and bean sticks, and a cleft hazel branch to prop my laundry line; willow for arches and structures; and pruned and windblown branches for kindling.

Opinions differ widely on the best wood for burning. *Grow your own Firewood* by Michael Littlewood discusses the choice at length and would make a good Christmas present for the fire-starter in your family. I love fruitwoods from the orchard, like apple, pear, cherry and plum that burn well with a pleasant flowery smell, but ash, oak, beech and blackthorn burn best, followed by hornbeam and birch. Walnut logs scent the air, while alder, elder, poplar, willow and lime should be burned mixed with other wood. Avoid

conifers which emit a clogging resin pitch that blocks flues. The poor old horse chestnut, currently beset by so many diseases, heats well, but spits.

When I'm feeling up to it, I'll stack my delivery of kiln-dried logs off the ground on a pallet base, with a sloping corrugated Onduline roof that keeps the wet off, but allows air to circulate. I'm never sure whether bonfires are a good thing. I'd never burn leaves – far too valuable composted as a soil conditioner, but a once-a-year clean-up of dead and diseased small wood on a brisk windless winter's day, once my cough is better, is a cathartic seasonal pleasure.

The ash from a bonfire or a wood-burning stove is rich in potassium and can be spread round fruit trees, sprinkled on the compost heap or heaped into the dust-bathing pit under the henhouse. Logs that are unsuitable for burning should be left in piles around the garden for creatures to over-winter. Gardens are an important sanctuary for wildlife, especially during winter months. I use this as an excuse to leave my garden undisturbed till spring.

12th

Jacques gets to see all sorts of interesting houses as he woodworks his way around Whitstable. He's been telling me, with great enthusiasm, about his latest project, building cupboards in an Eco Perch that the customer has had built in her parents' garden. She has moved from a spacious penthouse flat on the top floor of a 60s block in Brighton.

Her parents are in their eighties and live in a small house here, with an average-sized garden, and a pool, which they have converted into a fabulous swimming pond.

They applied for a certificate of permitted development, because the Eco Perch is compliant with the Caravan & Mobile Home Act and sits on a 6 metre by 8 metre footprint. Built of prefabricated panels lifted in by crane, it's a beautifully made curved pod, with wooden slats, timber lining and cedar shingles, reminiscent of a boat (have a look on blueforest.com). The building has an integral raised timber deck and folding sliding doors, perfect to take in Whitstable's stunning sunsets. She told me that living in such a small space with her terrier was challenging, but it's a healthy challenge, and her parents' life has been made easier and more pleasurable. A stylish solution to the problem of helping independent people through life.

Blue Forest make all sorts of tree houses, but their design team will produce bespoke buildings to your specs, taking care of planning issues. Prices start at £20,000. Wouldn't mind ending my days in such an elegant space, on terra firma at the bottom of someone's garden.

13th

Bravo! The builders have finally broken through the roof, fitted the bay window and the new bathroom space is there for all to see, in a fabulous new light that bathes the whole of upstairs, and can even be seen from the front door. The plumbers and tilers are fitting their bits and then Martin will come and add his magic. He'll build a sink cupboard and bath panel from old doors, add a wide shelf under the window and fit two etched glass sliding door panels. Max is coming down to help with the decorating and finishing, and the lino floor layer is booked for the end of the month.

Celebrate by dealing with a basket of quinces donated by a friend. These are great yellow boulders of fragrant fruit, and the thought of peeling and chopping them has been loitering in the back of my mind for a few days now. They look and smell so perfect on my blue starry Indian tray, but some are beginning to bruise, and if I'm not careful they'll be past it before I've lifted a finger.

I turn on the oven to medium and just pile them into my roasting pan, leaving them till their flesh is soft to the fork, then it can be scraped off the skin, and the core – conveniently intact – can be removed. I spoon the lovely yellow flesh into small plastic containers and freeze them, for use later as stuffing for the goose, filling for mince pies, as a compote under a crème caramel, and a delicious little extra for any apple dishes cooked over the next few months.

Medlars can be baked in the oven as well, and then eaten with teaspoons like tasty little boiled eggs with a blob of cream, and a sprinkle of cinnamon and brown sugar. Don't wait till they're bletted to eat them this way. With fruits like giant rosehips, medlars are pretty trees with giant leaves and lovely flowers.

Crab apples need to be made into jellies with plenty of sugar (equal amounts of strained juice to sugar). Delicious with a little chopped chilli. I tried turning them into membrillo or cotignac, with the same quantity of sugar, standing stirring by the stove till they were reduced, then sieving to remove the skin and cores: hard work, and only just worth the trouble.

Orchard fruit purée left over from jellies can be turned into fruit leathers, poured on to cling film lined trays a few centimetres thick, then baked

in a very low oven for six or seven hours, and cut into intensely flavoured squares.

Crab apples are ornamental trees, with blossom loved by bees; they act as pollinators for some varieties of apple, with brightly coloured fruits that are irresistible to birds like waxwings, and good autumn colour. *Malus* 'Royal Beauty' has dark red fruits with bronzy foliage, 'John Downie' fruits are almost edible straight from the tree, 'Evereste' has red and yellow striped apples and 'Golden Hornet's yellow fruits stay prettily on the tree all winter.

15th
To Cheltenham, on a slow train through the Cotswolds, to interview this year's Gardening Against the Odds winner: the Butterfly Garden, an educational gardening and land skills charity run for students of all ages and disablements by founder Chris Evans. I was deeply moved by the help and respect given to a lovely group of people, and imagine that everyone who visits – customers, staff, volunteers and even passing visitors like myself – leaves feeling better. This is how care in the community should work, but it needs enablers like Chris to make it happen, and he's a very rare bird indeed, who has given his life to those in his care.

17th
It's a busy time of the year for family birthdays, and with mild weather, it seems wimpish not to wrap up warm and celebrate out in the garden or on the beach in the gloaming.

This weekend we mark the naming ceremony of our newest family member, Ludo, with the planting of a tree – a tiny walnut seedling that hitched a ride from Suffolk, courtesy of the squirrels, in a pot of agapanthus. If your wildlife is not as accommodating, buy walnut 'Broadview'. It is precocious, producing large numbers of nuts from three years of age. Maybe those with large families, and equally large gardens, could plant a whole nuttery?

What could be better than a collection of nut trees, each reminding you of a member of your family? Some, like the almond, produce fragrant blossom, delicious-smelling kindling, and in milder areas, a harvest of nuts ('Robijn' stands the best chance); others, like the walnut, produce handsome timber, recipe potential both sweet and savoury, and fragrant leaves you can use in pot pourri. Sweet chestnuts with cross-hatched bark give us marrons glacés and their flour is used in lots of French dishes; and the native hazels give us garden supports, wildlife habitat a-plenty and pralines.

To make praline, one of the most tempting sweets in the world, first roast your nuts in the oven at 140C/275F for 20 minutes. Then carefully melt 125g caster sugar in a pan till golden, add 50g nuts and a squeeze of lemon juice, mix, then spoon on to greaseproof paper to cool. Break into pieces or blitz into a powder, and use to top ice creams and crumbles.

273

My friend Katy Cox of Mighty Fine Things makes cardamom, vanilla and almond praline, and chocolate-coated walnut and chilli brittle and one of her biggest sellers is chocolate and hazelnut vodka. Combine 250g chocolate and hazelnut paste (or Nutella) with 700ml vodka in a screwtop jar. Shake regularly and stir occasionally till the paste has dissolved into the alcohol. Strain carefully and bottle. Refrigerate and drink within a month.

For a winter party treat, try this chocolate, chestnut and cardamom cake. Melt 150g dark chocolate in a bowl over simmering water. Beat together 5 egg yolks with 150g caster sugar, then fold in 50g of ground almonds, the melted chocolate and a teaspoon of ground cardamom. Fold in the stiffly beaten egg whites and spread the mixture evenly on a greased and parchment-lined Swiss roll tray. Bake for 20 minutes at 180C/350F, then take out and leave to cool covered with a damp tea towel. Turn out on to greaseproof paper dusted with icing sugar.

To make the gooey filling, blend together 285ml whipped cream, 225g chestnut purée, 2 tablespoons dark brown sugar and ½ teaspoon ground cardamom and spread onto the cake. Roll your roulade carefully and serve dusted with lots of icing sugar.

Planting conkers, nuts and acorns with small children is always fun. Comparing heights and measuring up is the stuff of family legend, and my grandson will have plenty of walnuts if the squirrels don't get there first. The huge oak at the bottom of the garden was planted by the builder of this house, and has reached its centenary with a girth of 100 inches. Walnuts do better if planted small, so here's wishing Ludo and his tree a fabulously prolific future.

Different trees have specific meanings: plant oak for strength, olive for peace, crab apple for love, wild pear for loyalty, and rowan, the Celtic tree of life – to welcome a new baby. Birch symbolizes renewal, willow – imagination and vision, ash brings wisdom and hazel creativity. To preserve family unity, avoid hawthorn – it augurs contradiction.

To beat the cold and dark, we light the firebowl to keep us toasty, and roast chestnuts on its grill. Our party is lit by spluttering candles, safe inside hurricane lamps, and indoor sparklers that turn any occasion into a celebration, and we eat steaming hot mushroom soup followed by slices of Ludo's other grandma's walnut cake washed down with local sparkling wine.

Wild mushroom soup is made with soaked dried mushrooms, or with some of the more exotic varieties, like shitake or enoki, that can be grown at home from plugs popped into logs. Finely chop 2 garlic cloves, a couple of shallots and a leek. Fry gently in oil and butter till soft. Add 225g chopped mushrooms and fry briefly. Add 850g vegetable stock and a sprig of thyme, and simmer for 30 minutes. Adjust seasoning and strain through a fine-meshed sieve, liquidize, add single cream and sprinkle with thyme leaves.

Ailsa's walnut cake: bake a basic sponge with added chopped walnuts. For the luxurious filling: beat together 500g mascarpone and 85g light muscovado sugar and 4 tablespoons of Tia Maria. Use to sandwich and cover the cake. Decorate with toasted or caramelized walnut halves.

18th
My open larder emits the same cosy rosy glow for me, as my teenage sons used to get from the fridge, which they opened as a matter of course

every time they walked through the kitchen. Recently, I've noticed many of the shelves are groaning with my attempts to turn hedgerow and garden produce into alcohol, some dating back to 2004, my earliest vintage of sloe gin, but quince brandy, raspberry vodka, blackberry brandy, walnut liqueur, and my favourite rhubarb vodka all stand in rows waiting to be drunk. To be truthful, I rarely sit down to an evening of heavy spirit drinking, though I notice levels dissipating somewhat after visits from sons and friends.

Take a wide-mouthed jar that has been through a dishwasher cycle, fill half full with the fruit of your choice, add a quarter of granulated sugar (or more if you like your liqueurs sweet), then top up with alcohol of your choice. Brandy is rich and smooth, but gin and vodka have little inherent taste, and the French produce 'alcool pour fruits' (see www.uvinum.co.uk) with no flavour at all that allows the flavours of the fruit to dominate. Add a vanilla pod, cinnamon stick or twists of citrus peel for extra kick.

Recently I've been experimenting. Gin gets its particular taste from a combination of botanical flavours, predominantly juniper berries, but a dizzy online race through the new artisan gins' ingredients from sea pink to honeysuckle, heather to milk thistle, will make your head swim, so why not mix a cocktail from your herb garden.

Pour 500ml gin in a jar. Add a combination of tiny amounts of the following: juniper berries, rosemary, pine

276

needles, angelica stems, lavender flowers, crushed black peppercorns, elderberries, bay leaves, coriander and fennel seeds, and twists of citrus peel without the pith. Leave to macerate for a week in a cool dark place. Strain, bottle and drink iced, and experiment.

Stagger out before dusk to feed the hens their night-time feed of a handful of mixed corn, a good, slowly digested meal that'll see them through the night. I feed each one on a flowerpot saucer, which can be popped into the feed bin when finished, leaving no leftovers for unwanted diners.

24th

Ill again. Having spent the last few months with a large portion of my roof off (albeit under a scaffolding tent), acoustically – even downstairs – the effect has been a bit like actually sleeping in the garden. I've spent sleepless nights listening to every creak and shriek, squawk and twitter; at least I now know my garden a little better. I'm on intimate terms with the dog fox as he snuffles and quietly calls his vixen, who responds with shrieks and caterwauls that would raise the dead; I pity my poor robin as he starts his dawn chorus at 2am, woken by over-effective street lighting, and probably shortens his already tiny lifespan of just one year, and sympathize with all who experience winter weather in the raw.

Gardens give us a unique opportunity to see a working ecosystem: visiting birds, butterflies, insects, invertebrates

279

and mammals all live in their beds and borders, in orchards and vegetable plots. Mine has introduced me to a new circle of wildlife acquaintances: farewell to moles – thanks to the intractability of solid clay soil; sadly fewer frogs and toads, but joy of joys, hello to some shiny pale bronze slow worms; a nod in the direction of a murder of magpies (though not as murderous as we fear, according to the RSPB), and of course, a fearful shudder as a poultry keeper in my new relationship with foxes.

Friends and family might be shocked by my admission that my thoughts sometimes turn to gardener's revenge, as I watch the pigeons strip my fruit before it ripens and pesky squirrels scoff every walnut. Others may share my dark thoughts as Peter Rabbit nibbles their lettuces or Bambi ravages their roses, and many turn murderous at the mere thought of rats and moles.

I'm not suggesting you eat all these garden pests; near starvation wouldn't tempt me to roast squirrel or rook pie, but pigeon, venison and rabbit are delicious meat, and after a good life stuffing themselves with the fruits of your labours, this would seem a fitting end. In truth, I couldn't harm a fly, but I can get my own back by dreaming up a few recipes.

Even supermarkets stock farmed venison and rabbit, while many country butchers sell woodpigeon breast, plump on stolen corn, that can be quickly pan-fried in walnut oil and crushed juniper berries with chopped shallots and redcurrant jelly, and added sliced and still warm to an autumn salad of chicory and rocket leaves.

Game is available from farmers' markets, good butchers and shooting co-operatives. With lower fat and tastier meat, try venison or wild boar at Christmas; wild mallard cooked with whole clementines, partridge stewed in cider with fried apples, or stewed pheasant joints wrapped in bacon.

Alternatively, you could catch your own, as food historian Dorothy Hartley suggests in her *Food in England* (still available in hardback). She writes, 'Pheasant is fairly common in England in summer, when the cock invades the cottage garden to sneak the peas. You catch him quietly with a paper bag and raisin. Smear the paper inside with treacle, put a few raisins at the bottom, and prop the bag up amongst the peas. When he sticks his head in, he cannot see where to go, so he stands till you fetch him.' Think not!

27th
Max has been decorating the bedrooms in time for the flooring to be laid. Am fondly surprised by the extent of his handyman skills, recognizing his father's abilities. He's planning to take on and convert a wreck of a house in Walthamstow in tandem with his sound engineering and DJ gigs. So this is all good practice. We paint the walls and woodwork in sandstone – a creamy off-white that seems to reflect the other colours in the room, so that although almost the whole house is painted this colour, each room has a different atmosphere. My bedroom is slightly darker – the colour of the inside of a brown paper bag, with furniture painted the same pale blue and mauve as the sitting room. Wonderful to be hanging paintings that have been stacked for ages: seeing them again is like catching sight of them for the first time, and falling in love with them again. It's definitely a two-man job, with much standing back, assessing and faffing about. We develop a system and, finally, all friends' and family's works of art are hung.

Clothes that have spent months in boxes are released, shaken and then reassessed. Some will not be hung in my smart new wardrobes. A friend will take them and sell them on eBay, and the rest will go to the charity shop. Some need altering and mending, and these are put into a pile, and I fondly imagine myself sitting at my machine in my new sewing room, turning all these rarely worn clothes into everyday wear again.

28th

Feeling a little better, and I'm determined to be ready to open for the pop-up shop next week. Watching my cat on the stairs examining the customers as they filed into our first Whitstable Christmas shop, my sons said they could imagine her saying, 'But you promised we weren't going to do this anymore.' True, I'd vowed never to get involved in any more complicated retail events – my final Suffolk Christmas lasted for ten days and was even creeping upstairs, when the whole house was turned upside down, when the family had nowhere to sit, for ever longer portions of the year, and the house was turned into Santa's grotto.

But I swear this is Christmas Lite, with just a few friends coming to sell their wares. But three years on, we have already expanded into two houses, are selling mulled wine and biscuits for charity, and the invitation and marketing is causing multiple headaches.

I just can't resist buying at antique fairs and car-boot sales; I just can't stop myself making endless pressed leaf wreaths; I need to sell the leftovers from my Suffolk stock, and I love meeting new customers. I am a shopkeeper at heart.

DEC*ember*

1st

Christmas comes at exactly the right time of the year – just when we need cheering up and distracting from the cold, the dark and in my case, the inadequacies of my home decorating skills, along come all the distractions necessary to get us into a festive mood.

First, I must jolly up the house in time for our pop-up shop. I like to drape a small garland across the new fireplace, strung from a length of twisted florists' wire. I start with a loop at either end, and then select physalis lanterns speared with copper wire and tie one at each end – I like a bit of symmetry. Working inwards, I add small bunches of pearly papery honesty discs, teasels sprayed copper, some rosehips, a cone or two, some crab apples and for the first time this year, the seedheads of scabious 'Pom Pom' – its name says it all. You could string together citrus fruit slices dried in a cool oven with bunches of herbs, nutmegs and cinnamon sticks for a sweet-smelling garland.

I still make indoor wreaths from dried leaves glued onto florists' wire frames, criss-crossed with sticky tape, and love those that remind me of particular gardens. A visit to nearby Mount Ephraim produced deep purple, heart-shaped *Cercis canadensis* leaves, with yellow ginkgo and silver-sprayed bay leaves; a friend's garden produced a cache of fig leaves; and I've celebrated the oak tree at the end of the garden with a wreath of oak leaves and gilded acorns. I have my Barbie moments too, this year with a circlet of bright pink skeleton leaves with a few crystals, some bright red acer leaves and honesty discs.

Some homemade decorations will be a fleeting memory, fading long before Twelfth Night and the season's end, but others will survive to become part of your Christmas ritual, tucked away in a spare room to be brought out again, then given a quick make-over, ready to shine again. I have a mammoth *Allium schubertii* seedhead that made its way here from Suffolk in the car with Max, the cat and I, and now has pride of place hanging in my new porch.

This year, I thought I'd ring a few changes and made a journey across the Kent Downs, through lanes decked with seasonal berries, to Sissinghurst and a wreath-making course given by friends Jen and Becs from eco-florists Blooming Green for my *Telegraph* column. We were taught how to make a woven base from different coloured willows and dogwood stems, and decorate it with garden berries, hips, fruits, cones and dried flowers. There were baskets of dried hydrangea florets and pink gomphrena flowers, larch twigs covered in lichen and cones, dreadlocks of dried amaranth and multi-hipped clusters of rose hips to choose from.

My wreath looked stunning against my blue front door, protected in the porch, welcoming visitors, and as my berries lost their punch, I replaced them with other elements – like a garden pinboard. Scarlet berries from *Cotoneaster lacteus*, pink and orange spindle berries, purple callicarpa berries, apricot *Cotoneaster* 'Exburiensis' or red *Sorbus sargentiana* all make mind-altering coloured decorations.

2ⁿᵈ
At 10 o'clock we open our doors to the good people of Whitstable. I was lucky early on to discover Pascale, a

neighbour who cuts my hair and doubles up as a brilliant wooden decoration maker, and one day as she was snipping away we decided to open our houses at Christmas to sell our wares, asking other local makers to join us. The previous two shops have been a success, but there's always a niggling worry that no one will come.

The mulled wine is warming on the stove, the table is laden with good things to nibble, and we have a baker and a chocolatier, a woodcarver and an embroiderer, a purveyor of jams, condiments and fruit alcohols, and me, selling in one house; and decorations, antiques, cupcakes, and lavender bags chez Pascale.

Once it's all set up and selling, I love occasions like this. It's a great way to meet new people, greet friends and make a little money at the same time. My buys at the car-boot sales: 60s dolls' furniture, toys, French leather postman's bags, kitsch cut glass, 50s pottery, old tools, plus the usual books and leftover Kitchen Garden stock sell like hot cakes, and there's a little less stored in my attic. A good day for all of us, and as usual I've spent most of my profit at the other stalls, so my Christmas present list is sorted.

3rd

A glut of tiny artichoke buds from Macknade's bargain counter has encouraged me to pickle some in oil. I have been preserving vegetables in jars of olive oil for ages, as I imagine Italian peasants have done for centuries. Now,

293

because our houses are warmer, it's considered a bad idea to preserve food this way for more than a few weeks in the fridge. I still have jars in my larder that I'll eat, but I suggest you make small portions, enough for a meal or two. The rest could be frozen.

Trim the outer leaves from small bud artichokes, cut off their stems and scoop out their fluffy chokes. Cut them in quarters, then pop them in a bath of lemony water to stop them discolouring. Boil them in a mixture of one part vinegar to two parts salted water till tender. Drain well, then place in a sterilized Kilner jar and cover with oil heated with a few peppercorns, bay leaves, lemon slices, salt to taste and some sprigs of thyme. Seal when cool, making sure all the artichokes are under the oil. Keep in the fridge.

Mindful of health and safety, I've made just enough for us to eat over Christmas and strung the rest sprayed gold in a garland across my kitchen window.

6th

As you pile on the layers before going out into the garden, spare a thought for the birds that share your plot. Many small birds like wrens and tits roost together to keep warm, so clean out nest boxes and roosting pockets and secure them tightly, facing away from prevailing winds. Evergreen climbers, especially ivy, make perfect overwintering accommodation for birds, so leave them to flourish on trees and fences.

My early morning route to the chicken run is muddy and so I've laid down some wire panels on the grass path, a strip of underlay along the decking to make it a little less perilous, and laid a few paving stones in front of the feed bin. The run itself has been covered in a comfy layer of bark chippings. Hens are well insulated with fluffy duvets of winter plumage, but no one likes to stand in a howling gale, so a few strategically placed straw bales are just the ticket. If we suffer weeks of snowy weather, then a shelter built from bales with an old door as a roof will give your flock a chance to leave their henhouse, but still be undercover.

Turn their house round so the pop hole faces away from the wind, and insulate the inside with extra layers of newspaper, but make sure it's changed regularly to avoid the bedding getting damp. A hearty breakfast of wholemeal bread moistened with hot water or leftover porridge topped up with pellets will set up your flock, and remember to replace their water several times a day if it's really icy, in a container that's easy to knock out if the contents are frozen – a plastic bowl works better than the usual metal poultry drinkers.

During a really cold spell in Suffolk a few years ago, I traipsed through thick drifts to reach some new hens that were penned separately in a winter wonderland in a far part of the garden. After my third or fourth journey, I decided to bring these pullets into my conservatory to save myself the effort, and keep them safe. It worked brilliantly, I laid newspaper on the floor, built sleeping quarters out of a large cardboard box, and then eager to give them all mod cons, I stupidly offered them dustbathing facilities in an old drawer full of wood ash. Within seconds my whole conservatory, and later my whole house, was covered with a fine layer of white dust, just like Miss Havisham's rooms, as the whole flock enthusiastically dipped, dived, shook and flurried themselves in an orgy of preening.

The last few winters I spent in Suffolk were really cold and living down a one-track cul-de-sac in the middle of nowhere, we were snowed up for ages. I felt particularly cut off as my winter driving skills are pathetic and the car I had at the time leaked, so I'm relieved to be nearer civilization here and less at the mercy of the car.

8th

What reminds you most of childhood Christmas? Perhaps it's sights and sounds, but I bet for many its memories are evoked by scents and smells: of pine needles and tangerine peel, of chocolate and cheap eau de cologne, but happy times can also be evoked by spices, adding colour and depth and pungency to childhood souvenirs: cloves and coriander, dill seeds, ginger, juniper, mace, nutmeg, paprika and saffron – a sensual litany, the spice of life.

Spices have always been key ingredients in global trade, shaping the growth and downfall of many trading ports. Columbus, Marco Polo and Vasco da Gama's explorations were all condiment-based; wars were fought and throughout the centuries the strongest nations controlled the spice trade. Nowadays, the US is the world's major buyer, followed by Germany, Japan and France. Because I was brought up in Germany, gingerbread has a strong hold on my heart. I love gaudily decorated gingerbread men and their icing-laden houses, chocolate-covered lebkuchen and soft Italian amaretti, and sometimes bake these spicy biscuit decorations that are pretty enough to hang on the tree.

Mix together 225g plain flour, a teaspoon of ground ginger and 2 teaspoons of mixed spice – best to mix your own blend – with 100g butter and 100g caster sugar, then slacken with a beaten egg and a little milk. Blend to a smooth elastic dough. Chill in the fridge for 30 minutes and roll out ½cm thick on a floury board. Cut out in heart, star or other festive shapes and decorate with pink peppercorns, juniper berries, cardamom seeds or star anise.

Bake at 180C/350F for 15–20 minutes until pale brown. Remove from the oven and make small holes with a knitting needle or skewer at the top of each biscuit while they're still warm. Cool on a wire rack, then thread ribbon or shiny wire through the holes and hang them on your Christmas tree, or pack them in cellophane for stocking fillers.

Spice up your Christmas menu. Grate nutmeg into your mince pie filling with sliced preserved ginger; add crushed juniper berries, caraway and cumin seeds to red cabbage; sprinkle turmeric or saffron into mashed potato (and crushed allspice berries into mashed sweet potato), try juniper with game and cumin seeds with glazed carrots.

One of my favourite recipes is Natalie Hambro's tomato and cardamom jam that uses equal amounts of tomatoes and sugar, with a little lemon juice and ground cardamom seeds; and this one for muhammara, a fragrant dip to eat

299

with flatbread. Sauté a red onion in olive oil till soft. Process in a bowl with 60g walnuts, 3 roasted, skinned red peppers, ½ cup of pomegranate molasses and a teaspoon each of chilli, cumin and paprika powder, then blitz with a slice of stale bread and enough oil to make a thick paste. Season with lemon juice and salt.

10th

The first few Christmas cards. One or two from friends who've realized long-cherished dreams and moved abroad, to Italy and France. R adores her new life in a picture postcard *cascina*, has mastered the language and she and her partner are meeting like-minded people and making friends. The bureaucracy of the move, house conversion and building are a long-forgotten nightmare, and she loves *la dolce vita*.

N has never really learned to speak Italian and finds many of her neighbours, though kindness personified, have little in common with her, so she uses her house as a base and travels a lot, loving the country. Both say that their moves would have been difficult as single women, and making friends in the depths of the countryside would have been demanding. I know I'd have found it hard to make friends here if I were unable to speak English and with no connections.

But nothing is impossible, and though it takes more than a few sunny summer holidays to prepare you for life abroad, many have enjoyed the adventure. Having lived all over Europe, I'd recommend taking it slowly, spending time renting to get to know the area throughout the seasons, learning the rudiments of the language first, and choosing somewhere where you know a few people at least. If you don't have children or a job to help you make new friends, integrating can take a long time, though there are websites (like expatsinitaly.com) that can help with information and support. My sister-in-law moved to the south of France, and fell in love with the local butcher, a handsome and accomplished man, but it wasn't until she had mastered the past pluperfect that she realized he was a Le Pen supporter.

15th

A visit to Leeds Castle has ignited a real passion for Christmas trees in Ludo. Each room contained magnificent examples, including a mammoth tree in the entrance hall which reached up to the roof, covered in swirls of peacock feathers, that made up for the rather pathetic pair of huskies and reindeer advertised. All was put into perspective, though, by the small train that led us through the wind and rain from the car park to the castle: we can always rely on modes of transport for a real treat. Fire engines, cement mixers, tractors and helicopters are the key to a small boy's heart.

Back home to a favourite supper of baked beans and sausages. Have discovered a quick and easy homemade recipe that's predictably popular. Take a tin of tomatoes and fry with chopped leeks, adding a spoonful of muscovado sugar, one of pesto and salt to taste. Add a can of cannellini beans with a few tablespoons of crème fraiche and serve with good local sausages. With plum ice cream from the freezer, this is a favourite larder meal, loved by all generations of Raymond lads.

21st

Winter Equinox and the shortest day of the year. Things can only get better. Looking out of my bedroom window in the gloom of early dusk I contemplate my garden. There have obviously been changes, but because gardeners always look forward and not back, we concentrate on the future.

It's what keeps us all going. My plans to divide the garden into three sections: the bit nearest the house dedicated to entertaining with a veg bed, the central plot turned into an orchard and wildflower meadow with the chicken run, and the end bit left to wildlife and grandchildren have all come to fruition, and although this is no instant makeover, the framework is there.

24th

I try to leave most preparations until Christmas Eve, so the day is a surreal period of activity, calmed by the carol service from King's College on Radio 4. I make as many dishes beforehand as possible, our traditional spiced red cabbage and mixed root veg mash, which accompanies our roast goose stuffed with baked quince, keeps well, and my panettone bread and butter pudding – lighter and tastier than traditional Christmas pud, but equally festive – is better prepared the day before.

Early morning, soak 55g each of currants, sultanas and raisins in two tablespoons of rum and the zest of an orange and a lemon. In the evening, drink a celebratory glass of rum, then cut 280g of best panettone into thick slices. Brush a large pudding basin with melted butter and line with a layer of sliced panettone.

Whisk 3 free-range eggs (or 4 or 5 if you're using pullets' eggs like me) with 280g milk plus 140ml single cream and 55g light muscovado sugar, a scraped vanilla pod with

your rum and dried fruit, and pour some of the mixture into the basin. Put in another layer of panettone, then one of mixture until both are finished, ending with a layer of panettone.

Cover the top with greaseproof paper and weigh down with a couple of heavy tins. Steam for 2 hours and turn out, drizzle with a syrup made with the juice of a lemon and sugar to taste, then dust with caster sugar and decorate with lemon zest. We stick an indoor sparkler on top to bring this pud to the table with a flourish.

A few final decorations. My pyrotechnic efforts with artichoke heads and candles have been well documented – and often end with the comment to not try this at home, but the more daring reader might try to sink a nightlight or candle into the well made by snipping the choke out of a dried flower head, then watching it with an eagle eye. A safer candleholder can be made from little metal pastry cases or a cake tray tin called a bundt tin. It has a ready-made well in the centre to take a fat candle, and you can fill the surround with water and bunches of winter herbs: coloured sages, spiky rosemary, thyme and shiny bay leaves, to smell sweet and near to hand to use with Christmas dishes, so you don't have to trek out into the garden in the dark.

On our days out, Ludo and I have been walking up and down the High Street, minutely examining all the Christmas trees in every shop – the favourite is a strange artificial one with

305

snow that falls into an umbrella underneath the tree and is then magically swept upwards to mesmerically fall again. I'm afraid my sprayed twigs covered with little birds and fruit are not going to cut the mustard.

Just one last chore: to make chocolate leaves to decorate the pudding. Pick a dozen or so large bay leaves and brush their undersides with a little corn oil. Melt some good dark chocolate in a bowl over a saucepan of simmering water, then coat one side of each leaf and leave to dry. Carefully peel off the leaf and place on your pud, or leave them on a pretty plate with nuts and frosted grapes.

25th

Start the morning with scrumptious slices of cinnamon toast made with thick slices of brioche, toasted golden brown then spread with unsalted butter. Serve hot sprinkled with brown cinnamon sugar.

This is my third Christmas here in Whitstable. Max and his partner Helen are here for the holiday, so we open our stockings together and eat a late brunch of smoked salmon, washed down with a glass of fizz mixed with pomegranate juice – a fiddly procedure removing the jewel-like seeds from their membrane, but it's a pretty way to start the merrymaking (also good with tangerines). We are joined by the cat, who can smell the goose roasting and loves a family celebration. She is calm now, thanks to her daily medication, given today with a helping of goosemeat.

Jacques, Saskia, her sister Cait and Ludo arrive with bustle and excitement. How lovely to be spending the day with a child, sharing the frenzy of opening presents and the thrill of Christmas. I've been given a record player, and we spend time and giggles choosing from my ancient collection of albums, carefully stored since the seventies. The meal passes in a haze of booze, steam and delicious smells, playing with Ludo, and far too much to eat. We finish the evening scoffing leftovers to the music of Neil Young, Otis Redding and the Modern Jazz Quartet.

26t^h
To E's to spend the day watching films. She has installed a fantastic wide screen with surround sound, and there we sit encircled with bottles and nibbles on fat comfy sofas watching the latest movies, sometimes two or three back to back. After a day spent fighting the War of Independence with Lincoln; then sobbing as a beautiful lady dies in French, and learning to dance with Bradley Cooper, real life seems a little tame.

27th
Last decorating job of the year, to paint my stairs. A joy to remove the paint-spattered carpet and discover some battered but pretty stairs with all their mouldings. Max kindly abandons his buggy to remove a century of tacks, glue and dirt and we sand them smooth. Then I start a decorating conundrum, painstakingly applying layers of primer, undercoat, top coat and non-slip varnish in three colours to look like a stair runner. I can only paint each coat on every other stair, so that upstairs is still accessible, jumping up every other step, and pray that the cat understands the ploy. I use masking tape, only to find it strips off the basecoat as it is removed. Heigh ho!

31st
My task on the stairs has given me plenty of time to think as I end the year. Looking back, has it been a good move? Despite often missing friends, and occasionally suffering pangs of longing for the familiarity

of my Suffolk landscape, my house and garden and the life I used to have, I think it has.

I've made new friends and kept in touch with old ones. I have more time to enjoy exploring new panoramas and I'm gradually gaining a network of interesting people. I read more, will now listen to more music, and certainly watch more films.

I've enjoyed most of the building conversion – or more truthfully – the planning and the end result, and I'm beginning to love my new garden and hens. It's much easier to travel from here, and I enjoy walking and feel fitter. Three years on, I see more of my family, and have a close relationship with my grandson, whom I adore, and I'm sure I'll have as much fun with his eagerly expected sibling, due in the spring.

Who knows what the future will bring? But somehow, however hard the process, the fact that I've moved once, proves to me that I could do it again, if I had to. It takes away the fear of change, and that's liberating. Try it, if you have a mind to, if not, enjoy the life you have. We only have the one.

USEFUL WEBSITES

January

For farm equipment in Suffolk – clarkesofwalsham.co.uk

To visit The Leaping Hare in Suffolk – wykenvineyards.co.uk

February

To find your local farmers' market – localfoods.co.uk

My local farmers' market –whitstablefarmersmarket.co.uk

Best food shop in Faversham – macknade.com

Farm shop and home-reared butchers – monkshillfarm.org.uk

To find out about orchids and their care – orchid.org.uk

March

For those who keep poultry for pleasure – henkeepersassociation.co.uk

Good restaurant in Tankerton – jojosrestaurant.co.uk

Buying bulbs – gee-tee.co.uk and avonbulbs.co.uk

Visit Kensington Roof Gardens – roofgardens.virgin.com

Home of the National Fruit Collection – brogdale.org

Exotic fruit tree nursery in Norfolk – readsnursery.co.uk

For healthier plants with GroChar products – carbongold.com

Gardening Against the Odds – conservationfoundation.co.uk

Eco-friendly household paints – greenshop.co.uk

Franchi's vegetable seeds and products – seedsofitaly.com

Good range of vegetable seeds – mr-fothergills.co.uk

Organic gardener's catalogue – suffolkherbs.com

Year-round vegetable plants – delfland.co.uk

Wide variety of garden seeds – plant-world-seeds.com

April
Multi-sensory approach to herbs – invictaherbs.co.uk
Jacques Raymond – carpenter – moosejawwoodworks.com
Orpington breeder, all colours – keiths-orps.co.uk
For poultry breeders – poultryclub.org
Create your bespoke fragrance – jomalone.co.uk
Unusual veg and fruit seeds and plants – pennardplants.com
For wooden decorations – www.etsy.com/shop/miloumazou
May
Horticultural Therapy for veterans – gardeningleave.org
Roots to recovery for veterans – highground-uk.org
Wide and wonderful selection of irises – irisesonline.co.uk
June
Fruit growers mail order catalogue – pomonafruits.co.uk
Soft fruit and tree nursery – blackmoor.co.uk
Over 600 varieties of fruit & nut trees – keepers-nursery.co.uk.
July
Recycled fibre corrugated roof panels – onduline.co.uk
Lavender nursery – downderry-nursery.co.uk
High Street Whitstable restaurant – wheelersoysterbar.com
For information – whitstableoysterfestival.com
My builder James – whitstablebuilders.co.uk
For coastal gardens – seasideplants.co.uk
Lavender nursery – thelavenderg.co.uk
For beekeeping advice – bbka.org

August

Inspirational garden in East Sussex – greatdixter.co.uk
For succulents – blueleafplants.co.uk
Supplier of garden tools and ladders – niwaki.com
The Idler garden swinging seat – wilverley.com
Florist's supplies shop or online – wandmsmith.co.uk
Garden netting and gardening supplies – harrodshorticultural.com
Toby Schwenn Whitstable baker – slow-bread.com

September

Heirloom and heritage vegetable seeds – realseeds.co.uk
For information about cobnuts – kentishcobnutassociation.org.uk
Potash Farm range of nut trees – kentishcobnuts.com
Canterbury permanent farmers' market – thegoodsshed.co.uk

October

Faversham open house and gardens – mountephraimgardens.co.uk
Georgian house, garden and estate – belmont-house.org
English Woodlands trees and shrubs from ewburrows.co.uk
Catalogue and on-line semi-mature trees – barcham.co.uk
EcoPerch sustainable buildings and tree houses – blueforest.com

November

Advice on growing walnut trees – walnuttrees.co.uk
Nursery selling fruit and nut trees – ashridgetrees.co.uk
Delicious food from Faversham market – mightyfinethings.co.uk
Website selling French alcohol base – uvinium.co.uk
Handmade fruit liqueurs online – demijohn.co.uk

December

Eco florists and flower farm – bloominggreenflowers.co.uk
Herb plants online and courses – jekkasherbfarm.com
Spice shop on Portobello road and online – thespiceshop.co.uk
Faversham herb, flower and veg plant nursery – tastefulplants.co.uk
Nursery outside Canterbury – maytreenursery.co.uk
Garden centre Blean near Canterbury – meadow-craft.co.uk
For tempting cat treats – naturesmenu.co.uk
For blue egg laying hens in Kent – blue-egg-hens.co.uk
For chicken feed – allenandpage.com
For poultry equipment online – thepoultrysite.com

The Kitchen Garden *is an online shop for books, DVDs and information about courses on poultry keeping, gardening and cooking. We also open for the odd pop-up shop or special event. Keep up to date with our blog at* www.kitchen-garden-hens.co.uk

Join the Henkeepers' Association *Free advice, information and support for those who keep poultry for pleasure* www.henkeepersassociation.co.uk

INDEX